D1599132

Literary Criticism and Cultural Theory

The Interaction of Text and Society

Edited by

William E. Cain
Professor of English, Wellesley College

A Garland Series

Dissenting Fictions
Identity and Resistance in the Contemporary American Novel

Cathy Moses

Garland Publishing, Inc.
A member of the Taylor & Francis Group
New York & London
2000

Published in 2000 by
Garland Publishing Inc.
A Member of the Taylor & Francis Group
19 Union Square West
New York, NY 10003

10   9   8   7   6   5   4   3   2   1

**Library of Congress Cataloging-in-Publication Data available from
the Library of Congress**

Printed on acid-free, 250-year-life paper
Manufactured in the United States of America

Table of Contents

Acknowledgments

I wish to thank Deborah Clarke, without whose support, direction, and faith this book would not have been possible. Thanks also to Jennifer Jackson, Bernard Bell, and Christiane Makward, for all of their help, support, and patience. And, most of all, to Sunny and Lila Chirieleison, for their understanding and unflagging confidence.

Preface

Identity! My God! Who has any identity any more anyway?

—Young Emerson, in Ralph Ellison's *Invisible Man*

The question that launches Ellison's Invisible Man on his identity quest is more pertinent to the American novel now than it was when *Invisible Man* came out in 1952. The last quarter of the twentieth century has been marked by a developing skepticism about whether there is anything universal in the experience of being a woman, or a man, or an African American, or a lesbian, or a member of any other identity category once assumed to be universal—a skepticism reflected in the contemporary American novel. Chief among the questions this skepticism engenders is how resistance to racial, sexual, gender, and class oppression is to be effectively practiced if the individual subject can no longer assume her or himself to be part of a group with shared interests based on identity.

The culture of the sixties gave rise to the politics of identity: the notion that "the personal is political," that one's identity determines one's politics. Sixties identity politics produced the Black Power and later the women's liberation and gay liberation movements and served to mobilize large groups against racial, gender, and sexual oppression.

Within these groups, however, identity politics became problematic. The women's movement, for example, experienced severe schisms when it became apparent to working class women, to women of color, and to butch/femme lesbians that their interests were not represented under the rubric of "women" within the movement. The gay liberation movement is still responding to the fragmentation that came about when transgendered gays and lesbians demanded inclusion in the movement. It has become clear that monolithic identity categories like "women" and "gay" can no longer be assumed to be universal, and that such assumptions can be counterproductive to resistance practice. The women's movement of the sixties and early seventies, for example, contributed to the oppression of some lesbians, women of color, and working class women by claiming to represent all women while excluding these groups.

Resistance politics and practices based on notions of group identity, then, have proven unworkable. This conclusion would seem to position the individual subject in hopeless struggle against systems of oppression and domination. To further complicate the subjectivity question, the individual subject has, since the advent of postmodernism, been proclaimed all but dead.[1] And, in terms of the practice of resistance, the individual is assumed to be relatively powerless against systems and institutions of domination. This sort of thinking, however, assumes a fixed, hierarchical power structure with power at the top and the powerless at the bottom. Power relations, however, and their relationship to issues of identity, are now understood to be more complex and fluid than this model allows.

This book explores the production, deconstruction, and reinvention of identity in a selected group of novels that are among the most engaging of what I term "dissenting fictions": contemporary novels that critically engage existing political and cultural structures, creating fictional worlds that simultaneously indict and rewrite the power relationships they define. Specifically, I address narratives that are concerned with identity both as a multi-layered, shifting cultural construct (rather than as biological destiny) and as a vehicle for cultural critique, novels that talk back to specific, monolithic notions of essential identity. While they interrogate oppressive essentialist notions, many of these fictions yearn for a unifying essence that would encourage political solidarity (a lesbian nation, for example, or African-American community). This tension between resistance and unity is at the heart of the conflicts explored in these novels. Dissenting fictions are narratives of oppression and defiance that practice what bell hooks calls "critical resistance," narratives that "cultivate in everyday life a practice of critique and analysis that disrupt[s] and even deconstruct[s] those cultural productions that were designed to promote and reinforce domination" (*Yearnings* 3). My study is limited to narratives produced in the United States. The works differ in the components of identity on which they focus (race, gender, sexual orientation, class, and ethnicity, primarily), and in their strategies of resistance. I do not posit a unified strategy of resistance. At the close of the twentieth century, such a notion seems naïve at best. It is the notion that underlies the surge of nationalist politics that is sweeping the globe and taking its toll in human lives and dispossession. The exploration of the possibilities that lie within Foucault's idea of local and specific points of resistance is the work of the novels under study, and of this book. A focus on local and specific operations of power—grassroots resistance, in terms of praxis—is shared by all of the novels this book examines. In chapter one, I address the shifting meaning of subjectivity at the end of the twentieth century. In subsequent chapters, I proceed to close readings of the novels, focusing on the relationship between narrative, subjectivity, and resistance to oppression.

Notes

1.   I address this phenomenon in detail in chapter one.

Dissenting Fictions

Identity and Resistance in the Contemporary
American Novel

CHAPTER 1

Introduction:

The Dissenting Subject

> Power never concedes anything without a struggle. It never
> has and it never will.
>
> —Frederick Douglass

My exploration of identity in contemporary fictions begins with the
assumption that our identit(ies) are not determined by our anatomy, but
that anatomy can be seen as a point of departure from which we can
examine our differences. The novels in this study share a focus on the
human body. This book aims to interpret that focus in light of its implications for subjectivity, agency, and tactics of resistance to oppression.

The identity politics of the Black Power and feminist movements of
the sixties politicized the body with the rallying cry that "the personal
is political." As Alisa Solomon puts it, these movements "enabled us
to look at the most intimate phases of our lives and see the power relationships embedded in them" (27). As Greg Bordowitz points out,
though, identity politics now seem rooted in a "prior essentialist
moment," an historical moment in which "it was compelling to understand specific kinds of identity as essential to one's being, and to enter-
tain the fantasy of them being innate," a notion that now makes many
of us uneasy (Solomon 27).[1] The desire for a way to talk about identity that grants us a measure of unity but appreciates difference has
sparked a multivocal debate on the nature of subjectivity.

Previously unquestioned categorical identities—particularly those
based on gender, race, class, sexual orientation, and ethnicity—are

falling under increasing scrutiny. At the same time, we are discovering that there are limits to what can be said about who we are not—about culturally constructed identities—and we are beginning to look for new ways to define who we are. We are beginning to talk about taking the risk of positing some sort of inclusive reference point from which to define who "we" (women, for example, or lesbians, or African Americans) are. The task before us involves reevaluating the identity politics of the past and looking toward a future point beyond identity as it was once understood.

The acknowledgement of social constructivism is not the end of the story of identity. As Judith Butler argues in *Bodies that Matter*, the essence versus social constructionism binary is a constraint on productive thinking about identity. Butler's theory that identity is "performative," that the production of identity is not a single or deliberate act but a "reiterative and citational practice by which discourse produces the effects that it names" (*Bodies that Matter* 2) has been highly influential on contemporary thought about identity issues. In Butler's scheme of things, the subject is the product of specific restrictive normative frames. For example, the subject "becomes" a "girl" because the normative frame "It's a girl!" is reiterated through myriad speech acts and normative constraints (dress and behavior codes, etc). The possibility for resistance exists within the very reiterative frames that produce and regulate identity. "It's a girl!" can be reiterated as "It's a lesbian!" In the cultural necessity of constantly identifying oneself and being identified, the possibility of agency takes form. Hegemonic codes can be reprogrammed—repeated with a difference. Thus, according to Butler, dominant cultures produce what they exclude, what Butler calls "abject" or unthinkable bodies, the lesbian body, for example, or the transgendered body. "The abject," Butler asserts,

> designates . . . precisely those "unlivable" and "uninihabitable" zones of social life which are nevertheless densely populated by those who do not enjoy the status of the subject, but whose living under the sign of the 'unlivable' is required to circumscribe the zone of the subject. This zone of uninihabitability will constitute the defining limit of the subject's domain; it will constitute that site of dreaded identification against which—and by virtue of which—the domain of the subject will circumscribe its own claim to autonomy and to life. In this sense,

> then, the subject is constituted through the force of exclusion and abjection, one which produces a constitutive outside to the subject, an abjected outside, which is, after all, 'inside' the subject as its own founding repudiation. (*Bodies that Matter* 3).

But how, exactly, does social constructionism exclude as it produces identities? Dissenting fictions provide answers to this question. They affirm that identity is not something that is imprinted on passive bodies by monolithic social structures, it is a reiterative process of relations of identification between the body and social structures. There is no stable site for identity—even bodies are subject to change, but, as Butler contends, we cannot ignore the materiality of the body, the specificity of the excluded. Dissenting fictions focus on the materiality of the excluded, of the marginalized body in history and in resistance struggles. They perform a cultural analysis of the resisting subject. In dissenting fictions, resistance to culturally produced identities is not merely reactionary; it has its genesis in the body. Resistance, in dissenting fictions, is the result of the lived experience of actual bodies, and it necessarily involves the recovery of history and the constitution of interactive agency. In the next segment of this chapter, I extend my observations on identity production to Wilbert Rideau and Ron Wikberg's prison narratives, with the purpose of clarifying some of the theoretical positions I have taken by applying them to the highly constrained theater of gendered identity production within the penitentiary.

In *Life Sentences: Rage and Survival Behind Bars*, a collection of essays published in 1992, Rideau and Wikberg, who have served a combined total of fifty-four years in Louisiana's Angola State Penitentiary, describe and critique the world they have inhabited for the majority of their adult lives. The book is an eloquent response to our nation's rage for law, order, and longer and longer prison sentences. It is also a well-drawn portrait of the engines that drive the cultural production of gendered identity.

Rideau and Wikberg's unsparingly horrific description of the microcosmic all-male society that incarceration has produced—where old men languish in isolation, young rape victims are forced to "marry" their rapists, sexual slavery is the foundation of the economy, and "galboys" are the chief commodity—tells us as much about the stratified society outside of the penitentiary as it does about the one inside. The power relations that shape inmates' identities are explicit intensifications of those on the outside. The rigidly constructed identities brutally imposed upon inmates are amplifications of sexual, class-based, and racial hierarchies in what inmates refer to as the "free world." The identities produced by prison culture are exaggerated interpretations of the "essential" identities that outside culture produces. Gender, in the pentitiary, is highly self-conscious drag. Butler writes that "[i]n imitating gender, drag implicitly reveals the imitative structure of gender itself" (*Gender Trouble* 137). The reiterative "performances" that constitute gendered identity in the penitentiary demonstrate the constructed nature of essential gendered identities.

In prison, identity is imposed on the basis of appearances, as on the outside, but the protocol for identity production in prison is the reverse of that on the outside. On the outside if one's body is "female," one is imprinted with the identity of "woman," the characteristics associated with which include passivity, nurturance, sexual receptivity, etc.[2] In prison, if one appears to display those characteristics, one is identified as a woman (bitch, slave, whore, old lady). This reversal brings into question the notion that gender follows naturally from sex, the notion that, as Butler puts it, "'the body,' or 'the sexed body' [is] the firm foundation on which gender and systems of compulsory sexuality operate" (*Gender Trouble* 129).

In the penitentiary, the body is the site of identity construction. The obviously physically weak become instant victims upon entry into the penitentiary. They are reconstructed as "female," and, under threat of brutal rape, submit to somewhat less brutal "wifehood" and prostitution, from which their protector/husbands profit. When they are no longer desirable wives or profit-making prostitutes, they are cast off, and if they are lucky, they will be considered too old or infirm to be useful pawns in the ongoing power struggle. In the penitentiary's complex system of power relations, victim status, desirability, and commodification are almost entirely determined on the basis of the body's ability or lack of ability to resist the gendered identity that is reiteratively imposed upon it as essential. The only way to reconstruct oneself as a "man," during or after the initial attack(s) that define one as female and victim, is to defeat one's attackers. There are narratives, for example, in which the victim, after the initial attack which has resulted in his forced marriage to his rapist, stabs the rapist to death in a surprise attack. The victim then receives a sentence twice as long as his original one, and his willingness to accept these consequences prove him "crazy" enough to be useless as a commodity/wife. He thus avoids future attacks and reinvents himself as a "man," who will most likely become a husband/attacker/pimp. Wikberg and Rideau indict the system and the players that rigidly define identity in terms of what Butler would call the "performed" body and the culturally produced identities attached to it.

As Foucault demonstrates in *Discipline and Punish*, the Western cultural systems of discipline and punishment that predated the penitentiary were focused on "the body of the condemned," which was subject to a public spectacle of torture, dismemberment, and death. *Discipline and Punish* traces the evolution of the body-centered public punishment system into our "criminal justice system" that purports to believe in (mind-centered) rehabilitation, which ostensibly takes place in private, behind closed locked cell doors. In actuality, as *Life Sentences* forcefully demonstrates, the culture that thrives behind bars is almost entirely focussed on the body and has nothing to do with rehabilitation, except in extraordinary cases in which the prisoner is rehabilitated not because of the system but in spite of it. The violent inscription of binary sex identities on unwilling bodies in the penitentiary challenges the notion of the naturally "sexed [or gendered] body." Those who do not fit into one stereotypical gender category (male) are forced into the "opposite" category (female). The naturalness of both categories is thus brought into question. Those who brutalize others in the act of imposing gendered identities are themselves performing gendered identities that are no more "natural" than the feminized identities they impose on their victims. It must be noted, too, that some male inmates choose to express—and in some cases even profit from—a feminized identity.

Rideau and Wikberg's description of the manner in which identity is constituted behind prison walls supports two of Foucault's observations that are integral to the theoretical framework of my study of dissenting fictions. The first is that "power is 'always already there,' that one is never 'outside' it, that there are no 'margins' for those who break with the system to gambol in" (*Power/Knowledge* 141). In Rideau and Wikberg's world, there are ways to manipulate power, but there is no way to disengage from a relationship with power.

The second observation that I will address is Foucault's claim that "there are no relations of power without resistances." Resistance, for Foucault, is

> formed right at the point where relations of power are exercised; resistance to power does not have to come from elsewhere to be real, nor is it inexorably frustrated through being the compatriot of power. It exists all the more by being in the same place as power; hence, like power, resistance is multiple and can be integrated in global strategies. (*Power/Knowledge* 142)

The notion that resistance to power is not engendered in some pure space outside of power, that "[w]here there is power, there is resistance, and yet, or rather consequently, this resistance is never in a position of exteriority in relation to power" (Foucault, *The History of Sexuality* 1:95) is central to my critique of dissenting fictions. Dissenting fictions argue that we are not metaphorically imprisoned by power; we interact with systems of power, we resist, and in these interactions and resistances, our understanding of agency and identity is produced and transformed.

Current discourse on the nature of identity focuses on questions regarding what and how much we can say about the modernist notion of a universal subject. Many poststructuralist theorists see the very notion of subjectivity as problematic. Judith Butler questions "the viability of 'the subject' as the ultimate candidate for representation or, indeed, liberation" (*Gender Trouble* 1). Butler reiterates Foucault's proclamation of the death of the subject. For Foucault, a theory of unified subjectivity is untenable. In characteristically broad and sweeping terms, he demands, in a late interview, "a search for styles of existence as different from each other as possible" ("Michel Foucault: Final Interview" 12).

While most of us agree with Foucault that "different" "styles of existence" are to be sought out, addressed, and respected, we disagree on the degree to which cultural, racial, sexual, class-based, and other differences ought to separate us. What is being debated is the nature of the mechanisms through which identity is culturally produced, and the role of the subject in his or her own production. The question, in other words, of how we are to move from possible to actual resistance.

Postmodern theorists have proclaimed the nonexistence of the subject at precisely the moment when many marginalized subjects are asserting their voices and proclaiming their subjectivity as an act of resistance. "It never surprises me," writes bell hooks,

> when black folks respond to the critique of essentialism, especially when it denies the validity of identity politics, by saying, "Yeah, it's easy to give up identity, when you got one." Should we not be suspicious of postmodern critiques of the "subject" when they surface at a historical moment when many subjugated people feel themselves coming to voice for the first time? [3]

hooks goes on to answer her own question:

> The critique of essentialism encouraged by postmodernist thought is useful for African-Americans concerned with reformulating outmoded notions of identity. We have for too long had imposed upon us from both the outside and the inside a narrow, constricting notion of blackness. Postmodern critiques of essentialism which challenge notions of universality and static over-determined identity . . . can open up new possibilities for the construction of the self and the assertion of agency. (*Yearnings* 28)

The assertion of agency is, simply put, a conduit to power; it is the act of exerting power or resistance, of demanding and articulating a voice. Hooks points out that agency without essentialism is not only possible but desirable, that a speaking subject need not be a unified subject.[4] Groups or individuals who see their focal issues as related can address shared concerns without claiming or being limited by an essential core identity. Linda Alcoff writes, for example, that the "simultaneity of oppressions" experienced by women of color makes both essential gendered and essential racial subjectivity an impossibility (412). Belief in a core female identity, writes Trinh T. Minh-Ha, "does *not* . . . allow us to depart from the master's logic. It seems content with reforms that, at best, contribute to the improvement and/or enlargement of the identity enclosure, but do not, in any way, attempt to remove its fence" (Trinh 96). She calls for the dismantling of "the very notion of core (be it static or not) *and* identity" (Trinh 96, emphasis mine).

Trinh's distinction between "core" and "identity," and her call for the dismantling of both, imply a blanket rejection of identity. Sally Munt, speaking from the perspective of another subject that is often excluded from the category "woman," is a bit more ambivalent about the dismantling of core identity. Although she believes that "lesbian" is a social construction bound by culture and history, and not an essential identity, she is nostalgic for the simple subject of the past: "We need our dream of a lesbian nation, even as we recognise its fictionality" (xviii). The desire—however ambivalent—for agency without essentialism is manifested in the late twentieth-century overshadowing of identity politics by coalition politics.

My project is to unearth in selected contemporary novels a theory of dissenting subjectivity that takes difference—primarily racial, gender, and class-based—into account in more than an abstract and passing manner. Difference—the racial, class, gender, and ethnicity configurations operative in power relations—is precisely what Foucault glosses over in his treatment of fragmented subjectivity.[5] It is only in his final works that Foucault is at all interested in the specific features of the oppressed, and this interest is expressed primarily in his treatment of the "hysterization of women's bodies" in *The History of Sexuality*, an analysis that seems much more applicable to white, upper-class, Western women's experience than to that of working-class women, women of color, or Third World women.[6]

Although Foucault did not explore difference, he indicated a means by which it might be productively explored. In his final works, he shifted from a focus on power to a focus on lived experience.[7] He defines experience as "the correlation between fields of knowledge, types of normativity, and forms of subjectivity in a particular culture" (*The Use of Pleasure* 4). Our experience, then, is an amalgam of the culturally produced knowledge that we encounter; the rules and behavioral codes we are subjected to; and the manner in which, individually and collectively, we enact notions of essence (as black women, white women, gay fathers, etc).

My treatment of subjectivity has a triple focus: on experience, on difference, and on agency—on the role we play, or have the potential to play, in constituting ourselves as human subjects. By experience, I mean both lived experience and the historical experience of groups with which we identify. I agree with Elizabeth Grosz that "experience cannot be taken as an unproblematic given, a position through which one can judge knowledges, for experience is of course implicated in and produced by various knowledges and social practices" (94). But, as Grosz also observes, ". . . without some acknowledgment of the formative role of experience in the establishment of knowledges, feminism has no grounds from which to dispute patriarchal norms" (94). Experience plays an equally important role in resistance struggles that do not necessarily align themselves with feminism.

In exploring identity from a theoretical perspective, I emphasize the importance of the body. The body is, as Grosz notes, "the very 'stuff' of subjectivity" (ix). Essential notions of identity posit an essence of being that is intrinsic to the body (woman's "nature," for example). In exploring the function of the body in dissenting fictions, I explore identities that are inscribed on our bodies and *said to be* essential—I explore the production of "essential" identity. This production is brutally mimicked in *Life Sentences* when men who exhibit behaviors or traits traditionally associated with women are violently reinvented as "galboys." It would be a mistake, however, to view the body as a blank slate on which identity is inscribed. The body itself is a construct. Grosz argues that

> bodies cannot be adequately understood as ahistorical, precultural, or natural objects in any simple way; they are not only inscribed . . . by social pressures external to them but are the products, the direct effects, of the very social constitution of nature itself. It is not simply that the body is represented in a variety of ways according to historical, social, and cultural exigencies while it remains basically the same; these factors actively produce the body as a determinate type.[8] (x)

An acknowledgment of the specificity of bodies multiplies the possibilities for resistance. The specificity of the body allows us to move beyond a "continuum" image of identity (with male on one end and female on the other, for example) and into what Grosz calls a "field"— a multi-dimensional continuum that represents race, class, caste, and other "body specifications" (19).

Dissenting fictions portray power in Foucaldian terms—as "always already there," pervasive, and constantly changing, rather than in terms of hierarchies or binary oppositions (*Power/Knowledge* 141).[9] Although many contemporary fictions are engaged in the examination of power relationships and the processes through which identity is constituted, most envision power as distributed from the top down, not as omnipresent.[10] Dissenting fictions portray power relations in more nuanced terms, and in doing so they multiply the possibilities for resistance. The focus on the body, and on local and intimate power relations, allows the authors treated here to delineate and engage in local acts of resistance, to challenge power at the site where it is experienced, and hence to privilege experience while questioning the relevance of Western masculine experience to the lives of those it has marginalized.

In questioning the universality of Western masculine experience, dissenting fictions interrogate and revise patriarchal historical narratives. All of the fictions in this study incorporate history into resistance strategy. The trajectory of the identity quest in these novels (with the exception of Banks's *Continental Drift*) moves from an awareness of the self as an isolated individual to the formation of a resisting identity through the recovery of history and the construction of community.[11] History, then, is the conduit through which subjectivity, fluid identity, and interpersonal agency are accessed.

The novels by the five authors addressed in this study interrogate the role of history in the construction of the dissenting subject. They question the wisdom of relegating history to the status of marks on a page, the urge to "[get] out of history" (White). Patricia Waugh contends that feminism (which she equates with "women's writing") and postmodernism share "an awareness of the problematic situation of the contemporary writer in relation to historical actuality and fictional tradition," in other words, that both feminist and postmodern fiction problematize the relationship of the writer to history (6). Linda Hutcheon attempts to bridge the divide between the writer and history:

> To say that the past is only known to us through textual traces is not . . .
> the same as saying that the past is only textual. . . . Past events are given
> meaning, not existence, by their representation in history. (81-82)

Nancy J. Peterson responds to Hutcheon positively, but cautions that

> a historical position in postmodern culture necessitates the recognition
> that history is a text composed of competing and conflicting represen-

tations and meanings—a recognition that precludes any return to a naive belief in transparent historical representation or even in realism.
(984)

For writers of dissenting fictions, the fact that "history is a text composed of competing and conflicting representations and meanings" does not pose a problem, because they are writing out of traditions and cultures that have always been excluded from or marginalized in historical texts. They know that for the story of history to be told, competing and conflicting voices must tell it from multiple perspectives; that there never was one true authoritative history. Dissenting fictions put the story back into history, and they put the human body back into history's story. They are not traditional historical fictions, fictions that embroider narratives around historical "facts." They recover marginalized histories and employ multiple perspectives in the recovery process—as Morrison does, for example, with the silent march down Fifth Avenue in *Jazz*, and Bradley does, in *The Chaneysville Incident* with resistance to slavery and to the organized terror that is the lynch mob. These multiple perspectives, in dissenting fictions, tell the story, they become the story. Historical narratives and identity narratives—narratives that generate and respond to "who are we" questions—are intertwined.

Characters in dissenting fictions often attempt to escape from or alter the site of cultural identity production—be it the body, the family, memories of childhood, medical or juridical institutions, or the entire cultural milieu—in order to revise their identity narratives.[12] Since it is impossible to divorce oneself entirely from culture, they create imaginary and/or temporary spaces where identity can be examined and reconstructed. Hence we find *Jazz's* adult Joe fixated on his mother's open-air cave-home; Russell Banks's protagonist Bob, in *Continental Drift*, uprooting his New England nuclear family in search of the American dream and heading for disaster in a station wagon bound for Florida; Silko's characters constantly on the move; Bradley's John Washington holed up in a rural cabin sipping toddies with his father's ghost; and Feinberg's Jess at home only on her motorcycle.

Ultimately, all of these narratives come to an awareness of the body as the site where power relations are carried out and resistance has its genesis. Toni Morrison's *Jazz* features a male character in a mid-life identity crisis who is haunted by the memory of his mother, a woman whose body is the totality of her identity. She does not wear clothes or communicate or interact with other humans. Without enculturation and language, she is an animal, glimpsed running through fields and forests and identified by her scent. She is the *tabula rasa* of identity inscription—the central metaphor around which the novel's interwoven stories are arranged in a jazz motif—but *Jazz* also explores the means by which her body is *produced* as a blank slate to be filled with the desires and needs of others. Of all the fictions addressed in subsequent chapters, perhaps the most riveting, in its treatment of the relationship between the body and identity, is Feinberg's *Stone Butch Blues*. Growing up transgendered in the nineteen-fifties, Jess, the protagonist, experiences nothing of what is supposed to be the essence of femaleness. The narrative traces her struggle for acceptance as a "he-she," an inhabitant of the space between the rigid cultural definitions of maleness and femaleness. Confronted by the biological fact of her body, she chemically and surgically alters it, assuming a male identity, but she finds passing as a man as constricting as being a woman.

The epistolary form of *Stone Butch Blues*, in which Jess writes herself into being in a letter to a former lover, emphasizes another crucial component of dissenting fictions: a focus on the significant role of discourse in the production and maintenance of hegemonic power. At the center of many of the narratives treated in succeeding chapters, marginalized or unrecognized discourses challenge systems of power and control. Speech acts and writing function as fundamental acts of resistance. Leslie Marmon Silko's titular *Almanac of the Dead* is a text passed down through generations of women that both foretells and enacts the unraveling of Western patriarchal hegemony. Jess, in *Stone Butch Blues*, constitutes her subjectivity and denies object status through the act of speaking, as does the protagonist of David Bradley's *The Chaneysville Incident*, albeit in a radically different mode.

Dissenting fictions focus on identities forged in struggle. They posit a dissenting subject, a subject who is an agent in her (or his) own construction and who positions herself in relation to historical experience and current forces that would determine her identity. The dissenting subject does not act, however, or does not successfully act, as an individual agent. Dissenting agency in these novels is interactive and aware of the constraints imposed by social structures. The ingenuity of these works is in the ferreting out of local manifestations of power and resistance and relating these, as Foucault does, to global strategies of resistance. Dissenting fictions move beyond Foucault in their address of specific identity configurations involving race, gender, class, and sexual orientation, and in their recovery and deployment of history as a resistance strategy.

This book addresses the literary applications of Foucault's claim, in "On the Genealogy of Ethics," that since "the self is not given to us . . . there is only one practical consequence: we have to create ourselves as a work of art"—to the creation, in dissenting fictions, of a viable subjectivity. In chapters two and three, I read Banks's *Continental Drift* and Morrison's *Jazz*, drawing on Morrison's thesis in *Playing in the Dark: Whiteness and the Literary Imagination*, that racial whiteness in canonical American literature, from its earliest beginnings to its present, is constructed around and in response to a "dark, abiding, signing Africanist presence"—whether there are any African-American or African characters present or not (5). Morrison limns a whiteness that defines itself in response to a mythologized "not-me" and "not-free" Other (38) whose "duties" include "exorcism, reification, and mirroring" (39). Banks deconstructs whiteness as few white authors—or critics—do. He explores whiteness in precisely the terms Morrison sets up in *Playing in the Dark*, and he lays bare the dependence on the notion of the universality of white male subjectivity that forms the core of the cultural construct of white male identity. My focus in these chapter is on agency. In chapter two I explore Banks's argument that agency outside of an awareness of sociopolitical structures is futile, and that the liberal humanist notion of individual agency is untenable in the late twentieth-century (and perhaps that it never was workable). In *Jazz*, Morrison suggests that an interactive agency grounded in an awareness of history and of political and social structures is integral to successful resistance strategy. Morrison's characters develop fragmented identities around the memory of absent parents who function as tropes for significant moments in the history of African-American oppression and resistance. In chapter three I trace her characters' evolution as resisting subjects and agents in the constitution of their identities and their histories.

Chapter four continues my exploration of the centrality of discourse and history to resistance strategy in dissenting fictions, with a focus on racist oppression and gender issues in David Bradley's novels, *South Street* and *The Chaneysville Incident.* I address both the masculine identity quest and the notion of the gendered text. I argue that a conception of desire akin to that described by Hélène Cixous as a desire that does not stage "the movement toward the other . . . in a patriarchal production" is central to Bradley's work. I delineate in Bradley's male identity quest narratives a progression toward a critical point at which female desire moves from margin to center to direct the quest.

Chapter five explicates the interrelationship of personal, local, and state-level power relations in Leslie Marmon Silko's epic, *Almanac of the Dead.* This chapter focuses on class-based resistance strategies, and on the critical role of discourse—and particularly of narrative history—in the *Almanac's* resistance strategy. The chapter concludes with an exploration of the centrality of the human body to the *Almanac's* diverse array of interconnected narratives of resistance to the colonization of the Americas.

In chapter six I read Leslie Feinberg's *Stone Butch Blues* as both innovative gender theory and a complex dissenting fiction that functions as a manifesto for transgender liberation. I bring *Stone Butch Blues* into a dialogue with contemporary gender theorists, focussing on the work of Judith Butler and Kate Bornstein. Feinberg grounds Judith Butler's theories of gender as "performance" in the context of class struggle. Returning to a focus on the role of the body in historical discourse and in the constitution of the subject as a resisting agent, I read the novel as a crucial revisionist history of the cultural meaning of working-class butch-femme lesbianism. I conclude my study with a brief afterword.

Notes

1.   The article cited is a forum, facilitated and transcribed by Alisa Solomon, in which Bordowitz was a participant; hence I credit Solomon.

2.   Butler, Kate Bornstein, Martine Rothblatt, Leslie Feinberg, and others have recently challenged the usefulness of "biological" sex binaries, just as

social constructionist feminists before them challenged essentialist notions of gender. Rothblatt refers to "the apartheid of sex." Their challenge seems to me to be the logical next step in gender studies, and I take it up later in this chapter, and in detail in chapter five.

3.   Linda Alcoff asks the same question, but from a different perspective. She sees dangerous similarities between feminist poststructuralist theories of the subject and classic liberalism, which posits an essential attainable truth.

4.   Trinh T. Minh-Ha concurs: ". . . speaking nearby or together certainly differs from speaking for and about. The latter aims at the finite and dwells in the realm of fixed oppositions (subject/object difference; man/woman sexual difference) . . ." (Trinh 101).

5.   Foucault's *Herculine Barbin* addresses gender difference, but this attention to difference rarely finds its way into his theoretical works.

6.   Foucalt describes this process as beginning in the eighteenth and continuing through the nineteenth and twentieth centuries. The "hysterization of women's bodies," he writes, is "a threefold process whereby the feminine body was analyzed—qualified and disqualified—as being throughly saturated with sexuality"(*The History of Sexuality* 1:104). "Hysterization constituted the female body as innately pathological, and was (and is) the cornerstone of both medical and social practice.

7.   Particularly in the last two volumes of *The History of Sexuality.* Foucault acknowledges this focus in the introduction to *The Use of Pleasure* (4). David Couzens Hoy, in the introduction to his book, discusses the shift in Foucault's focus from power to experience in terms of the stages of Foucault's development (4).

8.   Susan Bordo's *Unbearable Weight: Feminism, Western Culture, and the Body* provides a lively reading of some of the cultural and historical factors that construct bodies.

9.   The category of dissenting fictions is not limited to the works of authors listed at the beginning of this chapter. It is a large, diverse, noisy grouping that spills over the boundaries I have tentatively drawn. Additional contemporary artists working in this mode include Marilynne Robinson, Kathy Acker, Louise Erdrich, Gloria Naylor, Gerald Vizenor, Toni Cade Bambara, Julia Alvarez, and Alice Walker.

10.   Kathryn Hume discusses this division and addresses a subgroup of contemporary authors she calls "control artists," who envision a "Manichean division between the power brokers and the oppressed," in her article on Ishmael Reed (516).

CHAPTER 2

The Unbearable Whiteness of Being and the Africanist Presence in Russell Banks's *Continental Drift*

> Many unusual phenomena now indicated that we were entering upon a region of novelty and wonder . . . . The darkness had materially increased, relieved only by the glare of the water thrown back from the white curtain before us. Many gigantic and pallidly white birds flew continuously now from beyond the veil . . . . And now we rushed into the embraces of the cataract, where a chasm threw itself open to receive us. But there arose in our pathway a shrouded human figure, very far larger in its proportions than any dweller among men. And the hue of the skin of the figure was of the perfect whiteness of the snow.
>
> —Edgar Allen Poe *Narrative of A. Gordon Pym*

Russell Banks's novel *Continental Drift* (1985) dramatizes the failure of the American Dream. The novel tells the story of Bob Dubois, an oil burner mechanic from Catamount, New Hampshire who migrates with his wife and two young daughters to the place that embodies the American Dream for the northeastern working class: the Florida coast. The Dream meets the fate in *Continental Drift* that it meets in most late twentieth-century fiction: a violent death. *Continental Drift* is as much about the production of racial whiteness and the failure of individual agency, however, as it is about the failure of the American Dream, and the two are intrinsically interrelated in this novel. Here, as elsewhere in his fictional oeuvre, Banks interrogates the construction of white identity against and in response to the notion of a racial Other. Banks is one of the few U. S. authors whose fiction overtly addresses the role of the white imagination of a black Other in the construction of white identity. His efforts at this endeavor have been largely overlooked. The novel argues that a dissenting subjectivity canot coexist with a modernist notion of individual agency.

Continental Drift is primarily Bob's story, but another story emerges forty-seven pages into the novel: that of Vanise Dorsinville and her nephew Claude, two young Haitians who join the exodus to Florida, sharing in the care of Vanise's infant son, Charles. Bob and his family and Vanise and hers head toward a vision of America, seeking to trade "a condition for a destiny" (345). The Dorsinvilles' story is told alongside Bob's in alternating chapters. In the final chapters, the two narratives converge in a tragic conclusion that is foreshadowed in the novel's first sentence: Bob drifts into a job ferrying illegal immigrants from the Bahamas to Florida and stands by while his Jamaican mate Tyrone forces fifteen Haitians into rough surf half a mile off the Florida coast when their boat is hailed by a Coast Guard cutter. Vanise is the only survivor of the tragedy. Bob makes a botched effort to assuage his guilt by returning to Vanise the money the Haitians paid for passage. He is stabbed to death by a gang of youths who steal the money.

Roughly one hundred and twenty of the novel's four hundred and twenty pages are devoted to Vanise's and Claude's story, and most of these focus on Vanise. The structure of the novel mirrors the dominant U. S. culture's focus on the white man's story: his news, his history, and his actions. Bob's wife and daughters are present in the text largely to develop Bob's character. Vanise's story, literally, in terms of the words devoted to it, becomes the "minority" story. In the novel's "Invocation," which invokes the blessings of Voudon loas on the author's task and lays out the plot, a voice which claims to be Banks' announces that what follows is "the sad story of Robert Raymond Dubois" (1). There is no mention in the frame narrative of Vanise or any of the black characters, except for a vague use of the word "blackness." In the novel's frame and structure, Banks foregrounds the white man's story and the class issues that are central to the narrative; in the juxtaposition of Bob's and the Dorsinvilles' stories, however, Banks deconstructs the very notion of universal white identity. Vanise, and Bob's African American lover, Marguerite, function as representatives of what Toni Morrison, in *Playing in the Dark: Whiteness and the Literary Imagination*, calls the "Africanist" Other against which white identity is constructed.

The construction of identity in response to an Other is as present in contemporary literature as it is in the nineteenth and early twentieth-century works Morrison discusses in Playing In the Dark, but little has been said about it, until very recently, in relation to the literary production of white identity. Whiteness has been taken as the universal against which the Other is constructed as different and racialized. As Molly Hite puts it, "'race' as a marker of social otherness is bestowed by dominant ethnic groups on other ethnic groups" (19). In *Playing In the Dark*, Morrison notes that whiteness is de-raced and universalized in proportion to the degree of racial blackness assigned to the Africanist presence in a literary text.

Morrison's observations in *Playing in the Dark* about the formation of white identity in relation to a "dark, abiding presence" (5), a "not-me" (38), are in some ways similar to Judith Butler's address of the formation of the subject in relation to the "abject" bodies of the excluded. In Butler's account of the construction of subjectivity in relation to abject bodies, those who are excluded from the domain of the subject serve a similar function to that of Morrison's "Africanist presence." Butler's abject bodies "constitute that site of dreaded identification against which—and by virtue of which—the domain of the subject will circumscribe its own claim to autonomy and to life" (*Bodies that Matter* 3). In both Butler's and Morrison's schemas, "the subject is constituted through the force of exclusion and abjection," as Butler puts it (*Bodies that Matter* 3). Morrison, however, addresses the racialized and gendered aspects of the Other, as well as the class issues that the 'Othering' process raises; Butler focuses on gender and sexuality and all but ignores race and class. *Continental Drift* highlights the problems inherent in conflating—or attempting to separate—these components. Banks affirms that the construction of racial whiteness is intimately bound to notions of masculinity.

Continental Drift interrogates the sort of "othering" strategies that Morrison identifies in *Playing In the Dark*. Embedded in *Continental Drift*'s tragic plot is a narrative of the construction of male, white, working-class identity formation in relation to the Africanist Other. Bob

Dubois's tragedy is that of the subject addressed by Morrison in *Playing in the Dark* and Butler in *Bodies that Matter*. At the core of Bob's identity is only a sense of lack, of what he is not: not-blackness and not-femaleness. His sense of subjectivity is entirely dependent upon his notions of the abject Other, which he generally perceives as black and female.

The most elemental attribute of whiteness is its invisibility, an emptiness at it core, which is intimately associated with its universality and superiority. Banks destabilizes the connection between the absence at the core of whiteness and a sense of superiority by foregrounding the absence and exploring his protagonist's sense of inferiority and his clumsy, unsuccessful attempts at employing notions of racial superiority and difference to bolster his ego. Bob's conception of agency is rooted in the bankrupt American individuality of late patriarchal capitalism. Banks emphasizes the limitations of a subjectivity that is dependent upon exclusion and effectively critiques both capitalism and the liberal humanist notion of individual agency.

Neither Bob nor Vanise and Claude are agents in the telling of their stories. The novel is narrated by a dispassionate third person voice, sometimes in the present tense, sometimes in a future tense that emphsizes the narrator's role as storyteller. Vanise leaves the rural Haitian hill country, and Bob leaves small-town New Hampshire, to seek an America that does not exist. Both Bob and Vanise are severely limited in their ability to act as agents. The difference between Bob and Vanise is that Vanise realizes the limits of individual agency. Bob imagines that he acts on his own behalf, outside of social structures, and that he can reconstitute himself as an American success story.

Bob, and Vanise's nephew Claude, attempt to construct for themselves the persona of a "man's man." Ironically, Claude, a child, is more successful than is Bob at this task. Claude kills the man who imprisons his sister in a bedroom above a Bahamian bar, and Bob kills a would-be robber of his brother's liquor store. The brutal nature of power relations and the limitations of individual agency are driven home to Claude when he is forced to flee his native Haiti and raped in the hold of the boat that transports him to America. He is made aware of his place within class structures and, at the time of his death by drowning, he has learned how to work within those structures, violently asserting his black masculinity to advance his and his aunt's journey toward America. Bob, at the time of his death, continues to exercise a stubborn allegiance to individual agency and a blindness toward the class structures that prevent him from achieving the American Dream. Vanise worships the *loas* of Haitian *Voudon*, intermediaries between humans and the divine who must be "fed" by their human *serviteurs*; Bob's *loa* is materialism.

As his life in Florida falls apart, Bob longs for the homogeneity and stability of New Hampshire, "the place where all the people were white and spoke the same kind of English and wanted the same things from life and knew more or less how to get them. (149). Exposure to the comparative racial diversity of Florida undermines rather than supports his sense of ethnicity and racial superiority:

> The black and brown-skinned people, the American blacks in the department stores and supermarkets, the Jamaicans and Haitians in the fields, the Cubans in the filling stations—these working people, who got here first, belong here, not Bob and Elaine. . . It's Bob and his family who are newcomers, and Bob is embarrassed by his lateness. He feels ugly in his winter-gray skin. . . (64)

Bob attempts to compensate for this sense of ugliness by continually reconstructing himself as racially superior, but he is overcome by feelings of inadequacy. Banks depicts the construction of whiteness, then, as a reiterative process: Bob constructs himself as racially superior, by claiming that people of color are "not Americans," and by romanticizing and exoticizing the Other, but the process repeatedly fails, leaving Bob angry, frustrated and out of place; hence the "drift" of the novel's title. In laying bare the nature and the futility of the process of identity construction, Banks employs Bob as a metaphor for the instability of the notion of white male universal subjectivity and of racial whiteness itself.

The novel's privileging of Bob's story over Vanise's functions as metaphorical commentary on the construction of a U. S. national identity. Bob is bedrock working class male last-quarter-of-the-twentieth-century America: reeling from the shift from a production to a service-centered economy, and from the slow crumbling of the patriarchal power structure; desperately trying to assert his masculinity and individuality in a world of unstable subjectivities; and unable to make the transition from the assumption of whiteness as a universal norm to multiculturalism. Unaware of these instabilities and of opportunities for transformation, Bob blindly pursues the American Dream. The only agency he can conceive of is the liberal humanist notion of individual agency. He sees his situation as that of man against nature, man against woman, and man against the forces of evil, injustice, and entropy. In the early tragicomic scene that sets Bob in motion for Florida, he is pitted as man against Sears. Needless to say, Sears wins out. Bob is the normative, well-intentioned subject defined by his relationship to the Other, embodied in Vanise. Although Vanise and Bob do not cross paths until late in the novel, she clearly embodies the silent unfathomable blackness against which Bob's subjectivity is constituted and is found wanting.

Continental Drift's omniscient narrator fixes Vanise in the same gaze that the U.S. trains on Haiti, and Banks critiques that gaze. Vanise is the Other whose flight toward America the U.S. government narrowly interprets as a "natural" move toward better economic circumstances rather than a flight from a brutal state apparatus. Vanise is silenced by the narrator and presented as an object for our pity, just as the hundreds of Haitians fleeing their island by boat were presented on the nightly news throughout the U.S. in the 1980s and early 1990s, prior to President Aristide's return. The fleeing Haitians were an indistinguishable mass of dark faces, usually shot from above, from the vantage point of the secure coast guard vessel or media helicopter. The speaking subject with whom we were invited to identify was a white, male government spokesperson attempting to create order out of chaos. The United States was constructed in this tableau as a benevolent, rational, patriarchal presence: white, male, stable, and confident.

Ferrying a boatload of Haitians to Florida, Bob looks down upon them from the captain's bridge and sees what white America saw on nightly news broadcasts:

> how astonishingly black they [a]re, *African*, he thought, and how silent and obedient, how passive . . . . A quiescent, silent, shy people who seem fatalistic almost, who seem ready and even willing to accept whatever is given them. (350-351)

Bob sees himself as "their opposite" and the Haitians as closer to nature (351). He sees them as the romanticized Other and decides that "they know something about themselves, about history, about human life, that he doesn't know" (351). They are "sexier . . . than white people" (351). Without exchanging a word with the group of Haitians that huddle under a tarpaulin on the deck of his boat, Bob divines all of this. The Other is infused with mystery, and Bob feels uncomfortable in his body and with his thoughts. The very mystery and unfathomability of the Haitians makes Bob's white body real, if only in terms of its inadequacy. By presenting Bob's unmediated thoughts and allowing us a glimpse into Claude's and Vanise's perspective, Banks critiques Bob's gaze and the unconscious process through which Bob reiteratively constitutes himself as a subject in relation to what he perceives as the abject bodies of the Haitians. Banks lays down an additional layer of complexity: in gazing upon the Haitians and perceiving them as sexier and more knowing, Bob perceives his own body as abject, as excluded from knowledge and desire: he sees the abject "outside" inside himself.

To Bob, "black is presence and white is absence" (351). This perspective simultaneously inverts and upholds Ellison's notion of black invisibility. Bob sees the Haitians, but he sees what he wants to see. In what Bob imagines as the Haitians' passivity, his own agency is constituted: he is the speaking subject, commenting on their passivity even as he profits from their desire to escape Haiti.

Like Haiti's body politic, Vanise's body is subject to repeated invasions by men representing patriarchal and colonial interests, most of them associated with official shipboard hierarchies of command. The confident sense of self that Vanise possesses when we first meet her is brutally and serially assaulted, yet she recovers her wholeness in rituals in the service of the *loas* and, ultimately, by seeking help within the community of Haitian immigrants.

At the novel's close, Bob unconsciously stages a final failed movement toward the abject body of the excluded: he gazes up at Vanise from below and sees her as a foil whose function, "when the white man presents himself, [is] to name him to himself" (417). Bob attempts to deploy the image of Vanise in a desperate attempt to bestow substance and subjectivity upon himself, and again Banks critiques this process—moments later Bob is murdered. He ceases to exist as a subject. *Continental Drift*'s achievement is not its characterization of Vanise; it is the straightforward address of the means by which Bob constructs a self—and is constituted as a subject in response to what he perceives as a black, female "not-me," "not-free" Other.

Early in the novel, Bob's childhood friend Ave instills in him a yearning for universal subjectivity, planting the seed of the American Dream in his mind when he shares with Bob a revered clipping of a whiskey ad. At home in Catamount in the dead of winter, debating the move to Florida, Bob describes the ad to his wife, Elaine:

> There was this handsome guy wearing his trousers rolled up to his knees and no shirt on, walking ashore on some tropical island. And he's got this case of Haig & Haig on his shoulder and a dinghy on the shore behind him and a nice forty-foot catamaran sitting out in the bay . . . . And you want to know what I said? . . . I said, 'That's me . . . (29)

Bob interprets the whiskey ad as "a letter from Hugh Hefner asking him to spend a week with the Playmate of the Month."

The Haig & Haig ad serves as a central metaphor throughout the novel. Bob's first job in Florida involves toting cases of whiskey, his second involves piloting a catamaran, running tourists and Haitians. The playmate materializes as a Marguerite, the black woman who becomes Bob's paramour in Florida. Bob's American dream, however, goes off course; it goes entirely awry. The American individualism he embraces involves no link to the past or to a community and no awareness of the constraints imposed by social structures.

Bob struggles to reconstitute himself as the self-made man in the whiskey ad. He fails to see that, in the economic system that the whiskey ad represents, he is almost as disposable as the Haitians his partner forces overboard when the coast guard shows up. He fails to perceive the class and race structures Banks makes explicit in juxtaposing of Bob's and Vanise's stories. Instead, Bob imagines a pseudo-mythic relationship to the Other that he expresses in metaphors of colonialism—a relationship in which the Other functions to constitute the universality of heterosexual white male subjectivity.

In the opening pages Bob realizes that "the trouble with his life . . . is that it's over. . . . He's thirty years old, and if for the next thirty-five years he works as hard as he has so far, he will be able to stay exactly where he is now, materially, personally" (45). Arriving in Florida, heady with the possibility of remaking himself, Bob sees rows and rows of black folks working in the fields, black folks working in stores and filling stations. Like many white Americans, Bob has grown up

> without having known a single black person well enough to learn his or her name, without having seen a black person, except on television or from a great distance, even when that person happened to be standing right next to [him] in line at the bank or in a cafeteria or on a bus. (63)

Now black people "seem up close and inescapably real, as if they are suddenly banging on the windshield, yanking at the door handles . . ." (64). In the scene in which he realizes that the black people "were here first, belong here," and feels "ugly in his winter-gray skin," he is filled with fear (64). Looking upon the Other, he realizes who he is, and it is not the man in the whiskey ad. He sees himself as a displaced working-class chump, with his family and all of his belongings heaped in and on a shabby station wagon. He is unemployed, out of place, and uncomfortable in his white body. His wife Elaine asks, "All those black people working in the fields and everything, they're not really Americans, right?" (64). And in Bob's worldview, they are not. In presenting Bob's epiphany of self-recognition, Banks constructs an impressive critique of the effects—on both black and white folks—of patriarchal, classist capitalism and the drudgery to which it condemns people who dream of a better life.

There are no black people in Bob's whiskey ad vision of the future. The Africanist presence in the whiskey ad is symbolized by the island, the terrain to be conquered, the "dark" continent the white man comes ashore on with his case of whiskey, the symbolic slaver waiting in the bay.[1] The island is the terrain that defines the white man—the successful conqueror—just as Florida, the land of opportunity, signifies possibility in Bob's worldview. During sex with Marguerite, the African-American daughter of a liquor store co-worker, Bob sees her as "a dark lush jungle . . . himself as a white boat . . . sliding easily onto the hot golden sands of a tropical beach . . . com[ing] forward onto her," colonizing her (111-112). Bob uses Marguerite's body to refashion himself in the image of the man in the Haig & Haig ad. His whiteness and his maleness are constituted in the symbolic conquest of her black body.

Banks does not stop, however, at this stereotypical representation of the constitution of white heterosexual masculinity. He deconstructs it by placing Marguerite in control of the process of their lovemaking. She repeatedly denies Bob the privilege of penetrating her body, the act that he imagines as the ultimate conquest. She instructs him in the practice of "outercourse" and she achieves orgasm without penetration.[2] This practice could of course be pleasurable for both parties, but Bob perceives it as a failure on his part. Bob is semi-consciously acting upon an awareness that, as Harryette Mullen writes, the black woman is "furthest from whiteness" and "therefore imagined as being also furthest from all the advantages whiteness has to offer in a racist-sexist hierarchy of privilege and oppression, in which the privilege of whites and males is based upon and unattainable without the exploitation and oppression of blacks and females" (73). Banks makes it explicit, however, that Bob remains unaware of the class structures that prohibit him from ever attaining the status associated with the man in the Haig and Haig ad. Bob is dimly aware, at least in the scene described above, that his whiteness consists of little more than a notion of superiority over a black Other, but he is unaware of the class structures that constrain what he perceives as the individual agency that will transform him from an expendable laborer in his brother's liquor store to the man in the Haig and Haig ad who controls the means of production

In the long chapter that chronicles Bob and Elaine's arrival in Florida and the unraveling of Bob's American Dream, aptly titled, "Making a Killing," Bob is able to refashion himself only to the point where he comes undone. When he attempts to remake himself, he finds he has nothing to work with, only a sense of who he is not and a Gatsby-like longing to be the man in the whiskey ad. He initiates the affair with Marguerite, believing that intimacy with a black woman will "expose him to depths and sides of himself he does not know exist" (262). White lovers have made him aware of "the woman in himself, but with [Marguerite], he has to "pay attention to the black man in himself as well" (101). What Banks is getting at here is a conception of what approaching the Other might entail. As Butler observes, "the subject is constituted through the force of exclusion and abjection, one which produces a constitutive outside to the subject, an abjected outside, which is, after all, `inside' the subject as its own founding repudiation" (*Bodies that Matter* 3). In literally embracing the excluded subject

(Marguerite), Bob is forced to pay attention to the "abjected outside" inside himself, the "black man in himself." This apparently involves losing touch with the white man in himself: as the affair with Marguerite progresses, Bob becomes less and less sure of who he is and more and more certain of his inadequacy as a lover, as a husband, as a father (though he rarely gives his children more than a passing thought), and as an American success story. His family grows poorer and apart.

Walking sullenly into the liquor store late one night after a rendezvous with Marguerite, Bob imagines Marguerite with another man, a black man with a "huge prick" having "wild, Negro sex" and smoking reefer (115). This imagined black man is apparently the man that Bob both fears and aspires to be, the "black man in himself." Lost in his thoughts, he walks into a robbery in progress and, in bumbling terror, shoots and kills one of the two black thieves. This scene is apparently the culmination of his "paying more attention to the black man in himself." Every pathology associated in the white American imagination (and media) with black men is deployed in the sequence of events surrounding the robbery. In order to reestablish the possibility of his becoming the man in the whiskey ad, to affirm his white superiority and his birthright to the American Dream, Bob must kill the Other. Although it could be said that he shoots in self-defense, he is thinking of race, not robbery. Along with the day's take in the cash register, the thieves demand a case of scotch, announcing their symbolic intent to co-opt Bob's whiskey ad vision of success. Before he gets his hands on the gun that will make him the conqueror rather than the victim in this scene, Bob's thoughts race to the subject of race. He sees the stand-off as black versus white, and thinks "I don't love the nigger girl, I never did, I just love you Elaine, you and my babies. I'm a good man" (119). Only moments before, sitting in his car outside the store, "the only thing he knows, he tells himself, is that he loves [Marguerite] . . . a Southern black woman" (114). With his life on the line, Bob reasserts his white male dominance by denying that he is the lover of a "black woman" and reconstructing himself as a white man who has simply taken advantage of the body of a "nigger girl." It is apparently this reconstitution of his white manhood that allows him to pull the trigger. As Mullen puts it in her discussion of the relationship of the black image to the white psyche: "the attenuated humanity of the controlled, repressed, rational, ambitious white male has to be augmented by the animal/child/

woman/black who stand [sic] in relation to it as dependent/inferior"
(83). In order to summon all of his manhood prior to shooting the robber, Bob must reconstruct Marguerite as the "nigger girl." He constructs the robber's accomplice, a black man, as a child as well, perceiving him as a wet-eyed "boy" and a "kid" emitting "the awful bawl
of a child," having defecated in his pants in terror after Bob shoots his
companion (120). Bob's white masculinity is tenuous indeed: it bal-
ances precariously on the smoking gun in his hand and the imagination
of the black woman and youth as dependent children.

Although everyone assures him that he did the right thing, Bob does
not feel like a hero after shooting the thief. Neither does he feel guilty.
He feels more confused than ever, and in his melancholy, he articulates
(or the narrator articulates for him) a yearning for a working-class identity politics: "He barely knows what part of the country he's in. He no
longer remembers why he came here, why he left the place where he
knew who he was, knew what he felt and why. . ." (149) Bob regress-
es first to childhood, then to infancy, "floating free of time, a man without memories and without plans, like an infant, conscious only of the
immediate present" (287). After shooting the robber in his brother's
"Friendly Spirits" liquor store, it seems that Bob's friendly spirit aban-
dons him. With the death of the robber/Other Bob loses his soul, just as
Vanise will later feel that she has lost her soul when the Haitians are
forced into the sea and her infant drowns. In her Voudon belief system,
an infant who dies before it has acquired a soul of its own steals the soul
of someone else, in this case its mother, when sudden death occurs.
Bob's and Vanise's situations differ in that Bob drifts soullessly,
unmoored by community, religious beliefs, or an ethnic sense of presence, while Vanise is taken in by a close-knit community that shares her
culture, ethnicity, and religious beliefs and arranges for a Voudon service to restore her soul. Banks builds an additional layer of irony around
the stereotypical notion that black folks have more "soul" than white
folks, a stereotype we know that Bob believes wholeheartedly. After
Bob renounces his affair with Marguerite and symbolically kills "the
black man in himself," he loses his "soul." He enters a state where
agency is irrelevant and "forces larger than one's self, like history, say,
or God, or the unconscious" are in control (289). From this point on,
the unrelenting forces of destiny propel him forward to his doom. Bob
perceives history as a naturalistic force beyond his control, a power to

which he has no access. Banks argues that history is incomplete without the narratives of folks like Bob and Vanise.

In failing to perceive the class structures that constrain his American Dream, Bob fails to the perceive the possibility of what Patricia Mann calls "interpersonal," "engaged" agency (4). Bob's conception of agency is a distillation of the liberal humanist notion of the individual as a rational free agent in the production of knowledge and truth. He can imagine only individual—not collective or community—action. In portraying this belief in individual agency as a tragic failure on Bob's part, Banks seems to agree with Michelle Burnham, who calls for a new way of thinking about agency, "other than in terms of an autonomous subject working against, rather than within, the structure" (62) As Mann suggests, "the exercise of agency is typically interactive, necessarily understood in terms of relations between two or more individuals." (14) Hence her use of the term "interpersonal." Bob does not perceive the possibility of acting interpersonally, as a resisting subject, within structures like ethnicity, class, or religion, just as he is not consciously aware of the entitlements or the burden of male privilege.

After Bob has taken up a position that precludes agency and resistance, the parallels between his story and Vanise's become overt. Both Bob and Vanise expect a change of site to result in a change of fortunes, although Vanise sees her move as taking her away from immediate danger and toward an uncertain future. Bob expects a change of site to result in a change of identity. Only in his dreams does he realize that he is moving from wage slavery to wage slavery. Before he leaves Catamount, he dreams that he is a Siberian prisoner, forever in transport, moving "from one place of confinement to another" (23). After the move to Florida, his family makes a series of moves to ever-smaller, more confining living spaces, finally taking up residence in a trailer park. Bob's employment situation undergoes a series of parallel transformations: he moves from a position in New Hampshire with limited possibilities of advancement to a string of increasingly tenuous and temporary jobs. We never know Vanise's dreams. We never get inside her head. Black characters are flat products of the white imagination: they are seen as Bob would see them.

Vanise's story seems to materialize out of Bob's dream of the Siberian prisoner. She moves, quite literally, from one place of confinement to another, from the hold of a boat, where she is raped, to an

abandoned shed, where she is raped, to a locked room above a
Bahamian bar, where she is kept as a slave by the bar owner, who
charges others for the use of her body. We never know how she feels
about her situation. Banks describes the pain and rage that Claude feels
when he is raped by the ship's crew, but the narrative silences Vanise.
The only actions Vanise takes on her own and Claude's behalf are offer-
ings to the *loas*. Ultimately, these serve her better than Bob's offering
up of his identity to the *loa* of materialism serves him. Vanise survives
the passage to America, her own hideous Middle Passage. She survives
being cast into the sea by Bob's partner in the Haitian-running operation; though she cannot swim and the seas are roily, she somehow
makes it to shore. Although it seems that her strength and will propel
her toward shore, she does not see herself as an individual agent. She
sees herself as part of a social structure that revolves around spiritual
practices and responsibilities to the *loas*. Her belief in the *loas* as agents
who intervene on her behalf supports the notion that social structure and
agency need not be oppositional categories.[3]

The tension between agency and its impossibility is never resolved
in Bob's narrative. Banks stresses that Bob's fatal flaw is his inability
to recognize the relationship between his subjectivity and the social
structures upon which it is dependent. He fails to realize that the identity he strives for, that of the man in the Haig and Haig ad, what Banks
calls the hypermasculine "man's man," is a social construction dependent on other social constructs such as race and gender. In setting Bob
up as a tragic victim of his belief in individual agency, Banks concurs
with poststructuralist theorists who advance the notion that, as Kathy
Ferguson puts it, a conception of identity as "produced or generated
opens up possibilities of 'agency' that are insidiously foreclosed by
positions that take identity categories as foundational and fixed. . . .
[Social] construction is not opposed to agency; it is the necessary scene
of agency" (133-34).

In the final pages, Bob is a bumbling, unwitting but not unwilling
agent in his own murder. His murder is the last in a succession of events
in which Bob's fantasies of pathologized blackness become reality as
black characters become criminal caricatures. Soon after his arrival in
Florida, Bob fantasizes that a group of "huge black guys" hack him to
pieces with machetes during a robbery of the liquor store (81). This is
perhaps a manifestation of his fears about the inadequacy of his pale

white body. It is also a foreshadowing of his murder by a gang of youths armed with knives. The young men, whom our narrator descibes not as humans but as "wolves,"

> [stab] at him until he falls . . . almost weightlessly, like a pale blossom in a storm of pale blossoms, filling the air with white, a delicate, slowly shifting drift through moonlight to the ground. (418)

Bob has sacrificed the Haitian immigrants to his own *loa*: materialism, and, finally, he is sacrificed to the same *loa*: he is killed for money. The way that Bob's death is described, his whiteness succeeds him, it outlasts him, it is all that remains of him when he is gone. Banks's use of the "pale blossom" imagery is precisely the sort of "figuration of impenetrable whiteness that surface in American literature whenever an Africanist presence is engaged" that Morrison explores in *Playing in the Dark* (32). Morrison observes that

> these closed white images are found frequently, but not always, at the end of the narrative. They appear so often, and in such particular circumstances that they give pause. They clamor, it seems, for an attention that would yield the meaning that lies in their positioning" (32-33).

Morrison offers Pym's final envelopment by impenetrable whiteness in Poe's *Narrative of Arthur Gordon Pym*; the "white frozen wastes" that conclude Bellows's *Henderson the Rain King*, and Hemingway's "unbelievably white . . . Kilimanjaro" as classic examples of this phenomenon (*Playing in the Dark* 58-59). In *Continental Drift*, as in these canonical works, whiteness outlasts or succeeds 'white' characters. The meaning that lies in this positioning of impenetrable whiteness at the close of these narratives seems to me to be twofold. First, it signifies that whiteness has been constructed as universal, normalizing, and monolithic: it is all that remains. Paradoxically, and secondly, since the figures of whiteness in these texts (including the snow of blossoms in *Continental Drift*) succeed or take the place of characters who are constructed as racially white, the figures of whiteness also signify absence. In *Continental Drift*, as in much critical discourse on whiteness, absence rather than presence lies at the heart of whiteness. Banks fleshes out this notion in Bob's thinking that black folks are sexier, more embodied, more soulful, and cooler. Banks interrogates the connection between whiteness and absence that many canonical works depict as mythic and unfathomable.

When Bob Dubois engages with an Africanist presence in *Continental Drift*, it signifies an engagement with one of two physical events: sex or death. Usually it is the latter, sometimes there is a combined meditation on the two. The whiteness that Bob leaves behind him signifies difference. We are left with an image of a delicate white flower set upon by a dark horde, the individual members of which are indistinguishable. In presenting whiteness as all that is left of Bob as he falls to the ground, Banks underscores the tragedy of Bob's falling back (literally and figuratively) on race as a universal identity construct. On the boat with the Haitians, Tyrone's Africanist presence signifies the immorality against which Bob imagines the possibility of his acting as a moral agent is measured. Tyrone *acts* to drown the Haitians, Bob fails to act to save them. Bob sees the possibility of reestablishing himself as a moral agent in returning the money to Vanise. He imagines that everything, including moral agency, can be bought and sold. In charting Bob's movement toward the abject bodies that define the limits of his subjectivity, toward what Morrison would call an Africanist presence, Banks skillfully exposes the process through which white masculine identity is constituted as universal, a process that, as Morrison observes in *Playing in the Dark*, is deeply embedded but rarely examined in canonical American literature.

Banks's characters' lives disintegrate when individual agency is exercised outside of an awareness of one's place in a political economy. Banks presents Bob as a flawed agent who fails to understand the social and economic forces at work in the shaping of his destiny. Banks sees Bob's situation as "a failure of imagination" ("The Search for Clarity: An Interview . . ." 48). "Bob," Banks asserts,

> doesn't imagine his own relation to the larger economy. Bob's substitute for a sense of community is a sense of himself as a consumer; he's victimized, but he participates in his own victimization. And the opportunities that he has to escape, when they present themselves, he declines to really imagine his life and take hold of it and change it. ("The Search for Clarity" 48)

Bob is dragged down by the materialism he privileges, just as the Haitian passengers on his boat are dragged to the bottom of the sea by their *loas*. Banks skillfully employs the language of individual agency ("participates in his own victimization . . . declines to . . . imagine his life. . . take hold . . . take charge") to underscore the failure of liberal humanist notions of individual agency

The terrifying, unbearable absence that Bob perceives at the heart of his 'white' identity compels him toward his demise—it is as though the absence itself is endowed with a sinister agency. Throughout *Continental Drift*, Bob unconsciously employs characters of African descent to define the limits of white masculine subjectivity. Banks critiques this process, making connections between the failure of individual agency and the notion of white masculinity as a universal subjectivity. Banks argues that fixed conceptions of agency and subjectivity constrain those who are constructed as subjects as well as those who are constructed as abject, excluded bodies. At the novel's close, whiteness remains a vague universal, defined by what it is not. The American Dream remains distant, mythic, and unattainable by the working class subject bound by notions of individual agency. *Continental Drift* takes up the challenge that Morrison lays out in *Playing in the Dark*. It overtly charts the white engagement of blackness, addressing the everyday practices through which whiteness is reiteratively defined as a universal and measured against a "not-me."

Notes

1. I draw here on the association of the island, in the white imagination, with the exotic, with Africa, and with its inhabitants: people of color. For a thorough treatment of the origins and evolution of this myth, see Patrick Brantlinger's "Victorians and Africans: The Genealogy of the Myth of the Dark Continent."

2. I borrow the term "outercourse" from the language of safe sex education. It refers to sexual practices that do not involve penetration.

3. Michelle Burnham's directive that we abandon notions of the autonomous subject as a rational free agent working against rather than within social structures seems applicable here. Vanise's faith in the loas provides what Burnham, after Harriet Jacobs, calls a "loophole of retreat," a resistance community that functions within existing social structures. Vanise is excluded from the category of the subject by the dominant culture and brutalized by agents of racism and sexism; however, unlike Bob, she survives to claim a place for herself within the social structure.

CHAPTER 3

Playing in History's Dark: The Struggle for Agency in Toni Morrison's Jazz

> That Justice is a blind Goddess . . Is a thing to which we
> black are wise. Her bandage hides two festering sores . . .
> That once perhaps were eyes.
>
> —Langston Hughes

The mandate that Toni Morrison offers her fictional characters recalls Emerson's *Self Reliance* and Whitman's *Leaves of Grass*: reinvent yourself; imagine your life, take hold of it, and change it. In Morrison's fictional universe, however, this mandate is not synonymous with the classical liberal humanist injunction to the individual agent. As we have seen in the previous chapter, dissenting fictions are well aware of the problematics of individual agency in the late twentieth-century. Given the current unmooring of patriarchal kinship relations and the instability of identity politics, individual agency no longer has meaning, except in terms of the psychic and economic interrelatedness of individuals. As Patricia Mann observes:

> As our vision of society comes to rest less and less upon distinctly binary gendered relationships, our sense of individual agency loses its patriarchal foundations. Individual agency will appear to wane insofar as it is strongly identified with its previous binary, gendered content (149) . . . . Notions of individual achievement and freedom are extremely conflicted today as a consequence of social transformation (151).

Agency in Morrison's fiction is intimately bound up with social transformation. Like Banks's *Continental Drift*, *Jazz* dramatizes the failure
of individual agency. *Jazz* takes up where *Continental Drift* leaves off,
in a sense: it insists upon alternatives to individual agency and universal subjectivity. The life that Morrison challenges her characters to
imagine is one that can only be brought into being through an awareness
of the relationship between agency and social structures, an understanding of history, and a sense of community. [1] Some of Morrison's
characters, the Breedloves in *The Bluest Eye*, for example, are unable to
respond to the challenge. In *Jazz*, Violet and Joe Trace ultimately rise
to the challenge of self-reinvention, but only at great cost: the life of
Joe's lover, Dorcas. Their identity struggles come directly out of the
experience of power relations, both historical and quotidian. *Jazz*
explores the conjunction of the two. Its characters, if they are to survive
and thrive, must act with an awareness of their positioning within social
structures. Agency and transformation are central to Morrison's work,
but their positive exercise is possible only within the context of community and with an awareness of a political economy. This chapter
examines the relationship, in *Jazz*, between identity, agency, and history, in an effort to build upon the previous chapter's exploration of the
relationship between agency and identity.

   Morrison's communities function as judge, jury, and chorus, weigh-
ing collective responsibility against individual freedoms. The conflict
between individual freedoms and membership in and responsibility to a
community is a central tension in Morrison's work and has been
explored in depth by critics.[2] Roberta Rubenstein sums up the nature of
this conflict:

> Traditionally, black communities have functioned as structures that
> sustain and preserve the individual, particularly in adversity.
> Morrison's narratives address the nature and forms of this connection
> between self and other, individual and group, that may ambiguously
> both shape people's values and impede their capacity to express them
> within the community's norms. (127)

In Morrison's fiction, the exercise of individual agency outside of the
context of community is usually dissipated in reification, "the transformation of all human functions and qualities into commodities" (Willis,

"Eruptions of Funk" 42n). *Song of Solomon*'s Milkman is saved from his descent into a reified life only by a female-guided journey into his past that culminates in his figurative, if not literal, death. Nowhere is reification played out so dramatically as in Hagar's fatal shopping spree in *Song of Solomon*. Hagar seeks to bring about in herself, through name-brand purchases, the same sort of transformation that Pecola buys with her sanity in *The Bluest Eye*, and Violet spends half a life yearning for in *Jazz*.[3] All of these characters desire lighter skin and the appearance of whiteness, and they struggle with their desire on the margins of communities that deny them membership.

In the course of the self-denying process of internalizing the master narrative that equates beauty and desirability with light skin and blue eyes, Violet fetishizes the character Golden Gray, whom she has met only in her grandmother's stories. Gray is not the only character in *Jazz* to be freighted with meaning by a character who has never laid eyes on him. Joe fixates on Wild, Golden Gray constructs an identity around hatred for his absent father, and Violet becomes obsessed with the image of Dorcas. Other characters are haunted by the memory of ancestor figures they barely knew: Violet by her mother's absent presence and Dorcas by her parents', for example. I examine the function of these absent figures and their relationship to African American history and individual characters' conceptions of identity.

Throughout Morrison's fiction, African American characters construct identities in response to absent or imagined figures who represent significant moments in African American history. The ghost of Sethe's murdered baby in *Beloved* is the most straightforward example of this phenomenon.[4] In *Jazz*, nearly every major character is orphaned and desperately searching the bone-yards of American history for an identity. As characters sift through childhood memories haunted by the pervasive presence of death and abandonment, identities are constructed, deconstructed, and recovered in response to constricting culturally produced notions of race and gender. Violet Trace develops an identity around a double lack: she is haunted by the stories her grandmother told her about a golden-haired boy and she longs to be "[w]hite[, l]ight, [and y]oung again" (208). She sees herself as the dominant culture sees her: as an abject body excluded from the category of the subject, which is constructed as white or light-skinned and masculine, and which she believes is embodied in Golden Gray. Like Sethe, in *Beloved*, she

recovers a sense of wholeness and self late in the narrative's action with
the help of an unexpected catalyst: Felice, Dorcas's best friend. An
absent mother figure—Wild—serves as the catalyst for the construction
of Joe's identity. The men in Jazz model themselves not after a same-
gendered parent but in response to a mother figure. Golden Gray's
search for his father leads to a mother figure: the pregnant Wild. As in
Morrison's earlier fictions, the search for a usable past embodied in a
patriarchal presence yields unexpected results.[5]

In *Jazz*, Morrison returns to a historical theme she addresses in several earlier works: the Great Migration North, from 1890 to 1920, in
which two million black people left the Southern farm for the Northern
factory.[6] Denise Heinze addresses Morrison's reconstruction of this historical movement in Jazz:

> . . . southern blacks by the thousands migrated to the industrialized
> North in search of a more secure economic future . . . . In *Jazz*
> Morrison analyzes the psychological lure of the City, which offers
> blacks a retreat from the capriciousness of white southern rule, but
> which also effects isolation and loneliness . . . . [She] attempts to
> reconstruct the complex set of factors that motivated black people to
> migrate to the city in the first place and those factors that compelled
> them to stay. (116-117)

Jazz explores these "factors" in the lives of Joe and Violet Trace. Their
struggles are struggles with individual pasts that are intertwined with
the historical movement of the Great Migration. As in Morrison's earlier works, history is articulated through the lives of individuals.

The historical moment that *Jazz* departs from and returns to in the
improvisational style that gives the novel its name is the silent march
down New York's Fifth Avenue on July 28, 1917. From July first to
third, 1917, violent white mobs terrorized East St. Louis, Illinois, killing
more than forty black people. The "riots," an eruption into violence of
white fear and hatred of black workers, were ostensibly touched off by
the employment of black laborers in a factory under government con-
tract. White residents and police roamed the streets beating and killing
black people and setting fire to their homes—the fate that befalls
Dorcas's mother in *Jazz*. Several of the victims died when they were
shot as they attempted to escape the flames. The silent march down

Fifth Avenue was a response to the slaughter in East St. Louis and to the mounting death toll from lynchings across the country. John Hope Franklin describes the silent march:

> Saddened and solemn in dark suits and summer hats . . . some 10,000 blacks mourning the East St. Louis massacre . . . march[ed] down New York City's Fifth Avenue to no other sound than that of muffled drums. The feelings of the marchers were made quietly and eloquently clear in banners . . . one . . . combin[ing] the opening words of the U. S. Declaration of Independence and its promise of equal rights for all with the bitter suggestion that the words do not apply to blacks. (*An Illustrated History of Black Americans* 100-101)

The drumbeats of the march punctuate Morrison's narrative at regular intervals, drawing the narrator back from her far-flung reverie on the City and into the lives of Violet and Joe and those whose lives they alter. Each character experiences the march—and the history it represents— differently. Thus, *Jazz* asserts that history exists in its multiple interpretations, and that multiple histories can exist in narrative form without competition or cancellation.

Joe and Violet's histories merge around the Great Migration. They initially migrate North to distance themselves from childhood ghosts. Joe, Violet, and Dorcas all arrive as orphans in what they imagine as the city of possibility. The deaths and disappearances of all of their parents are the direct or indirect results of the racist oppression they hope they have seen the worst of in the rural South. But the city dehumanizes people and destroys the sense of community they had in the South. In depicting the resulting strain on Joe and Violet's marriage, Morrison traces the effects of operations of power and resistance on individual lives.

Like Bob in *Continental Drift*, Violet Trace initially defines herself in terms of what she is not: light skinned and young (208). But Morrison's protagonists, unlike the white characters in canonical American literature she treats in *Playing in the Dark*, must ultimately either refuse this definition by negation or suffer disastrous consequences like those that befall Pecola in *The Bluest Eye*. The dominant culture defines Morrison's characters in terms of what they lack (whiteness, light skin, youth, social standing), and confronting this "lack" is

their primary task. Characters initially respond to this challenge by
struggling with the memory of an absent, significant figure who represents a traumatic historical moment rather than struggling directly with
the identity imposed upon them by the dominant culture.

The Violet of the early chapters suffers from a fragmented identity.
She occasionally falls into the "cracks" between the fragments. She is
the embodiment of W. E. B. Dubois's double consciousness, a self made
ever aware by the gaze of a dominant culture of its "twoness,—an
American, a Negro; two souls, two thoughts, two unrecognized strivings in one dark body" (Dubois, 45). Violet's consciousness, however,
is split into at least three fragments: she is an American, black, and a
woman, and as a result of being "gifted," as Dubois puts it, with this
fragmented consciousness, and disconnected with the community she
was part of in the rural South, she loses all sense of agency.

> She wakes up in the morning and sees with perfect clarity a string of
> small, well-lit scenes. In each one something specific is being done:
> food things, work things; customers and acquaintances are encoun-
> tered, places entered. But she does not see herself doing these things.
> She sees them being done. . . . Sometimes when Violet isn't paying
> attention she stumbles onto these cracks, like the time when, instead
> of putting her left heel forward, she stepped back and folded her legs
> in order to sit in the street. (22-23)

Here subjectivity ("herself") and agency ("doing . . . things") are simultaneously intimately connected and irreconcilably separated. When she
falls into the "cracks," Violet is unable to see herself as an agent, and
hence she is unable to function. But as she is drawn deeper into her
obsession with Dorcas's photograph, she comes to see something else.
The photograph of Dorcas is a central image in the text, a jazz refrain,
like the silent march down Fifth Avenue. Like the march, and like history itself, the photograph exists outside of the text. Morrison has trans-
lated into fiction the narrative accompanying a photograph of a teenage
girl lying in her coffin in James Van der Zee's *Harlem Book of the Dead*.
Deborah McDowell recognizes that "in the process of 'enlarging' herself, Morrison's narrator has reduced Dorcas to the dimensions of a
snapshot—a motionless image, fixed, aestheticized, frozen" (4).
Although Dorcas briefly speaks late in the novel, it is the silent, frozen

image of Dorcas that is etched in the reader's mind; the image of Dorcas as she is perceived by others. Violet initially sees in Dorcas what she (Violet) is not: "a young me with high-yellow skin instead of black" (97). But she comes to see in the photo what she is, as a result of her interaction with Dorcas's aunt and surrogate mother, Alice Manfred. Alice and Violet's relationship brings about the transformation of both. Each triggers in the other a renewed sense of loss and longing for the mother. Searching through their memories for their missing mothers,[7] Alice and Violet discover sisterhood, reinventing family, community, and identity in the process. A turning point in their relationship occurs when they simultaneously experience a powerful desire for the mother and an utterance rises from each woman's unconscious, creating a rapid-fire exchange:

> [VIOLET:] "Oh shoot! Where the grown people? Is it us?"
> [ALICE blurts out and then covers her mouth:] "Oh, Mama." Violet
> had the same thought: "Mama. Mama?" (110)

This reawakening of longing for an absent mother brings about in both women feelings of childlikeness and powerlessness, feelings that fuel each woman's fixation on the absent presence of Dorcas and the history Dorcas's image conjures up for each.

Violet's obsession with the photo of Dorcas is paralleled by a fixation on a somewhat less elusive absent presence: that of her own youthful body. Violet tries to create a larger body in an effort to create a larger self and a sense of agency (93). She equates a larger body with "power," and she yearns for the body she had when she was chopping wood and plowing fields—for her before-the-Great-Migration-North self. "I want some fat in this life," she declares, just prior to the above exchange with Alice (111), employing fat as a metaphor for power. Violet's youthful, larger body is an absent presence she seeks to reproduce, and the remembered full-hipped body represents for her a romantically idealized pre-migration moment in history. The paradox of this longing is underscored elsewhere in the novel when the harsh realities of Violet's family life in the Jim Crow South are delineated. In Harlem, Violet consumes milkshakes laced with Dr. Dee's Nerve and Flesh Builder:

the milkshakes . . . didn't seem to be doing any good. The hips she
came here with were gone, too, just like the power in her back and
arms. Maybe that Violet, the one who knew where the butcher
knife was and was strong enough to use it, had the hips she had
lost. (94)

Historical power operations are played out in individual lives and
inscribed on bodies throughout Morrison's work.[8] Power relations are
intimately concerned with the body, and relations of power have an
immediate and direct effect upon bodies, not just a trickle-down or
metaphorical effect. Violet remembers her young adulthood, in which
she inhabited a larger, more powerful body, as a time of independence
and newfound wage-earning power, a time in which she was attractive
to her then-suitor, Joe Trace.

Like the anorectic, Violet seeks to gain power and control by modi-
fying the dimensions of her body, and she associates agency, power, and
control with "*that* Violet," the one who stabs Dorcas. Susan Bordo's
work on the treatment and experience of anorexia nervosa is useful in
reading Morrison's narrative of Violet's experience of her body.
Although the bodies Bordo treats are "slender" bodies and the desire
she explicates is a desire to be thin, her observations elucidate Violet's
desire for a larger body. Bordo asserts that anorectic women seek to
gain power and control over their lives by reducing the size of their bodies. *Jazz* is set in an era when a fuller, more rounded female body was
idealized. Violet seeks to enlarge her body for the same reasons that
Bordo cites in the anorectic's desire to reduce. Bordo cites four components of Augustinian mind-body duality that are present in the
anorectic's perception of her body: "[1] The body is experienced as
alien . . . . [2] The body is experienced as *confinement and limitation*.
. . . [3] The body is the *enemy* . . . . [4] The body is the locus of *all that
threatens our attempts at control*" (144-145 Italics Bordo's). Violet
perceives her body in all of these terms, and she develops a fragmented
identity in response to her perceptions. There is the Violet who is in
control and there is "*that* Violet," as she refers to her other self, who acts
upon her unmediated desires and is hence out of control:

Where she saw a lonesome chair left like an orphan in a park strip fac-
ing the river, that other Violet saw how the ice skim gave the railing's

black poles a weapony glint. Where she . . . noticed a child's cold
wrist jutting out of a too-short, hand-me-down coat, *that* Violet
slammed past a whitewoman into the seat of a trolley four minutes
late. And if she turned away from faces looking past her through
restaurant windows, *that* Violet heard the clack of the plate glass in
mean March wind. (89-90)

In this passage, the Violet who Violet perceives as her "self" sees an
"orphan," a *child's* cold wrist, and herself as a passive, unseen object
caught in the gaze of strangers looking at something more interesting.
Everywhere she looks she sees lonely, fragile, parentless children; she
sees her childhood. *That* Violet sees the possibility of aggression, of
resistance, of agency, in each vignette. Violet envies the position of
power that she imagines "*that* Violet" occupies, and she envies her double's sense of pride in her actions and her lack of shame (94). At the
root of Violet's malaise is a perception of her other self as an agent and
herself as a passive object who is acted upon. She sees her body as an
obstacle to agency and subjectivity rather than as the site of a resisting
subjectivity. She sees her body as the black woman's body has historically been constructed by a dominant Other, and she does not, at this
point, see the possibility of a coexisting narrative history that would
construct her as a resisting agent.

Bordo notes that anorectics report a fear of hunger that is more
potent than their fear of becoming "fat." Violet's condition, too,
involves a fear of hunger: a fear of the hunger her mother experienced.
One of her strongest memories of her mother is of her drinking from an
empty cup.

> She didn't want to be like that. Oh never like that. To sit at the
> table alone in the moonlight, sipping boiled coffee from a white
> china cup as long as it was there, and pretending to sip it when it
> was gone; waiting for morning when men came, talking low as
> though nobody were there but themselves, and picked around in
> our things, lifting out what they wanted—what was theirs, they
> said, although we cooked in it, washed sheets in it, sat on it, ate off
> of it. (98)

Hunger here is literally associated with race and class oppression. The empty cup is both the result and the symbol of the poverty racism imposed on Rose Dear's family. Oppression, object status, and deprivation are figuratively bound up for Violet in the image of her mother's lean, hungry body. Her attempt to become larger is a symbolic act of resistance. What she has become, however, is more like the figure her mother became after she succumbed to poverty and racist oppression: smaller and silent, speaking only to her caged birds, and disconnected from her community.

Jazz is, in part, the story of Violet's merging of her two selves and recovery of her former self, the powerful, laughing, signifying young woman who chopped wood, plowed fields, and traded words with Joe Trace until sunrise. The narrative of Violet's recovery of her voice and reinvention of her self is not, however, a narrative of an individual agent remaking herself. The notion that she acts as an individual, outside of history and social structures, is precisely what Violet has to give up to become whole. Violet's story is a narrative that demonstrates the interrelationship of identity formation and resistance to oppression. Bell hooks addresses this interrelationship:

> Traditional therapy, mainstream psychoanalytical practices, often do not consider "race" an important issue, and as a result do not adequately address the mental-health dilemmas of black people. Yet these dilemmas are very real. They persist in our daily life and they undermine our capacity to live fully and joyously. They even prevent us from participating in organized collective struggle aimed at ending domination and transforming society. (*Sisters of the Yam* 15)

Hooks go on to affirm that in traditional Southern black culture, the well-being of the psyche was addressed by the church and the community, and mental health problems were "treated by the diverse and usually uncertified 'healers' who folks knew to take their troubles to" (*Sisters of the Yam* 16). In migrating from the rural South to the urban North, Violet leaves behind both the site of her childhood deprivation and the means to safely and effectively address it within a supportive community.

Just as Violet is haunted by visions of her absent mother, Joe is obsessed with visions of his. This obsession is the result of Joe's yearning for the sense of community he left behind in the rural South. Like Morrison's other characters who are cut off from community and thus from interactive agency, Joe constructs an identity around a lack: his mother's absence. Barbara Hill Rigney writes that, "for Morrison, the relationship with the mother is always ambiguous, revelatory, yet destructive, even for women, but the male desire to return to the womb, to reenter the mother, is often more negatively associated with a surrender of consciousness, or a death wish" (14).[9] Joe remembers his mother, Wild, as a lack, an absence, a barely glimpsed presence. For reasons that are not made clear, Wild rejects not only the infant Joe, but, before him, all of "civilized" society. She runs naked through the cane fields, making her home in a cave, and eschews contact with other humans. Like many of Morrison's other mothers, she may be read as a response to a whole range of stereotypical representations of the mother, and particularly as a response to canonical American literature's mammy figure, of which Faulkner's Dilsey is perhaps the most well known example. Faulkner's appendix to *The Sound and the Fury* states, "DILSEY. They endured." "They" are mammies, self-sacrificing surrogate mothers to white children: the African American mother as she was for decades portrayed in American literature. Wild does not endure motherhood, community, or social structure. She is the subject who refuses identity. Like the march down Fifth Avenue and the photo of Dorcas, the image of Wild's absent presence (in his searching for her, Joe finds only a scent and the flutter of redwing blackbirds) is a central metaphor around which *Jazz* is structured.

Although her history is sketchy, it is clear that just as Joe "chang[es] into new seven times" as a resistance strategy to violent racist oppression, Wild unmakes herself (123). She eschews human identity and its trappings, except in the safe space of her cave, which is described as womb-like (184). To reach Wild's cave, Joe must cross the Treason river, and getting to the river is in itself problematic:

> . . . to get there you risked treachery by the very ground you walked on. The slopes and low hills that fell gently toward the river only appeared welcoming; underneath vines, carpet grass, wild grape, hibiscus, and wood sorrel, the ground was as porous as a sieve. A step could swallow your foot or your whole self. (182)

The "treachery" associated with Wild is the fall down the dangerous slope from community and culturally constructed identity to its absence, the slope that "only appear[s] welcoming" and can swallow your whole "self." Wild's self, or at least the outward projection of it, has indeed disappeared, and the very earth surrounding her is fraught with danger. Wild is a figure of subjectivity entirely divorced from social structure. She is a fictional embodiment of the ideas Anthony Appiah develops when he argues that the problem with what he terms "structural determinism" lies in a mistaken belief that subjectivity and social structure (or society) are linked categories. Appiah sees the categories of agent and structure as separate discursive economies that are related but not inextricably so.

Michelle Burnham responds to Appiah's argument with the contention that "the problem is not, as Appiah has suggested, that the independent categories of subject and structure have been falsely wedded, but that the categories of subject and agency have been so" (62). She asks, "Why not refuse, then, the individualization of agency and its entrapment in the discourse of the subject, and posit instead an agency that operates within not only the discourse, but the very architecture of the structure?" (62-63). Putting her theory into practice, Burnham uses the example of Harriet Jacobs's slave narrative. Jacobs becomes an effective agent in securing her freedom by becoming both literally and figuratively a part of the structure of slaveholding society, hiding out in the middle of town in her grandmother's shed for seven years. She observes and manipulates the activities of her oppressors from behind a panoptic blind, all-seeing and unseen, an invisible member of the black community, which is aware of her presence in its midst while her oppressors seek in vain for her as far north as New York, misled as to her whereabouts by letters she has written and smuggled to friends in the North who posted them. Burnham argues that Jacobs is an effective agent because she works from a "loophole of retreat" within the social structure, where she is invisible to hegemonic powers but is a visible member of the resistance community. Burnham's stance on agency is similar to Morrison's in its accent on community rather than individual agency as an effective resistance response to hegemonic power. Wild's cave serves as a loophole of retreat outside of, rather than within, social structures. It is a complex signifying structure: a womblike structure inhabited by a mother who refuses motherhood, a stone womb that beckons to Golden Gray, and an empty space filled with history that haunts Joe's imagination.

Like Joe, Golden Gray has a mother who refuses to acknowledge him as her son. His father doesn't know he exists. Gray sets off on a mission to find and kill his absent black father, to kill the blackness in himself. But in a Morrisonian twist, his search for the father yields two nontraditional results: his identity is unraveled rather than reinvented and the classic patriarchal quest leads him to a mother figure. The first thing Gray encounters is the pregnant Wild—and I say "thing" because he sees her as less than human, as lower on the evolutionary scale than his horse. He sees "[b]lack & nothing," a "nigger," and instantaneously acknowledges there's "another kind of black" —himself—the human kind (149). Unable to reconcile his humanness with his blackness, Gray rushes toward a confrontation with his black father and with a history of miscegenation and secrecy.

Morrison interrupts Gray's volatile first exchange with his father with a scream from Wild as she enters the final throes of labor and is about to give birth. The narrative of the patriarchal quest for the father is replaced, almost mid-sentence, with a narrative that privileges the matriline. The reader's attention is refocussed, with that of the characters, on the opening between Wild's legs from which the infant Joe is about to emerge. Gray is symbolically reborn as a black man—his father acknowledges him as his son—at the moment of Joe's birth. Later, Hunter's Hunter admonishes Gray to choose: black or white, the binaries still presented at the close of the twentieth century to people of "mixed race" who have the option of passing for white. Gray rejects both options: "I don't want to be a free nigger; I want to be a free man" (173). His protected upbringing as a privileged white boy prevents Gray from understanding the implications of that sentence to his father, who has struggled all of his life to retain his dignity as a black man. His father's reply, "Don't we all," silences him. It also serves to close the narrative of Gray's quest for the father. Our narrator simply drops the patrilineal narrative and shifts our attention to Wild. Morrison subverts the dominant discourse on gender that privileges the patriarchal descent line, placing a problematic, unwilling mother figure at the heart of a male identity quest. The displacement effectively decenters Gray's quest for the father, which is apparently aborted.

The narrator offers only the vaguest clues as to what becomes of
Golden Gray after the day he confronts his father. We learn that thir-
teen years after Joe's birth, Hunter's Hunter encounters Wild in the cane
fields and has the eerie sensation that at the moment Wild touches him
on the shoulder, a pair of eyes is watching him from ground level, as
though Wild is not the only one hidden in the cane. We are told that
Hunter's Hunter speculates that Wild, like Violet, is "hungry" for "hair
the color of a young man's name," and that "to see the two of them
together was a regular jolt; the young man's head of yellow hair long as
a dog's tail next to her skein of black wool" (167). The implication is
clearly that rather than choose black or white, Gray has chosen the
"loophole of retreat" that Wild represents and that the two are glimpsed
together in the cane and the woods. When Joe enters Wild's chamber,
he finds Gray's clothes and toilet articles there. Their presence disturbs
him, and he "disrupt[s] things" in the chamber as a result, leaving it in
disarray, "chang[ing] it all to a way it was never meant to be" (184).
Gray attaches himself to the character he discovers in the search for the
father—a character who is neither a father nor a mother but rather a representation, to him, of the racialized and gendered Other. In taking up
with her, Gray effectively disappears from the text. Paradoxically, his
association with Wild implies his acceptance of his blackness and his
complete rejection of the very social structures that construct race. In
his movement toward Wild's abject body, Gray's subjectivity is subsumed by the abject. He becomes what Judith Butler describes as the
"abjected outside, which is, after all, 'inside the subject as its own
founding repudiation": he becomes what he has repudiated (*Bodies That
Matter* 3). His legacy, however, continues to torment Violet as the
memory of Wild torments Joe.

Through Dorcas, and later through Felice's ministrations, both Violet
and Joe find what they are looking for: they recover their capacities for
self-love. This process proves fatal for Dorcas but ultimately healing
for both Joe and Violet. Bell hooks writes that

> [s]ystems of domination exploit folks best when they deprive us of
> our capacity to experience our own agency and alter our ability to
> care and to love ourselves and others . . . . The choice to love has
> always been a gesture of resistance for African-Americans.
> (*Sisters of the Yam* 130-131)

Hooks asserts that "our collective difficulties with the art and the act of loving began in the context of slavery" (*Sisters of the Yam* 131). She addresses the assault upon the black family under slavery: the separation of families, the daily brutality, the necessity of dissimulation. Unlike contemporary white politicians and media figures who pass doomsday judgment on the black family and blame black mothers, however, hooks stresses the connections between self-love, the capacity to love others, agency, and resistance. These are precisely the connections that Morrison makes in *Jazz*. She explores what hooks calls "the choice to love" in all of its complexity. In interweaving the histories and struggles of her characters across generations and in merging Violet's and Joe's histories in the coming together of Golden Gray and Wild, Morrison stresses the interpersonal, interactive dimension of agency and resistance—at the expense of Dorcas, who is the victim of Joe and Violet's belief that they act as individual agents. Ultimately, *Jazz* argues for what Patricia Mann calls an "interpersonal," "engaged" agency (4). *Jazz* suggests that, given the current instability of subjectivities and identities, we should focus on our actions and not on fragile, unstable notions of selfhood.

In the novel's final pages, the narrator addresses the construction of agency directly in an implied dialogue with the reader that focuses on the reader/writer/text relationship. In a particularly mean-spirited review, Bruce Bawer finds the narrative voice "a bit *too* rich, its general effect that of a somewhat too heavy perfume. Its frequent descent from vibrant authenticity into glib detachment muddles one's image of the narrator . . ." (11).[10] Bawer's demands for an "authentic," reliable narrative voice seem at best anachronistic, but they are worth considering because they are precisely the demands that the narrator overtly refuses to meet in the final pages. As Denise Heinze points out,

> Jazz [is] a metafictional fiction that commits the supreme transgression—it calls into question the very authority of authorship. [Morrison] effects this with the use of a narrator as enigmatic and ghostly as Beloved and possessed of a similar feminine, African-American consciousness, the difference being that the uncanny, or that which should remain secret, is not a collectively repressed national disgrace, but *a collectively dormant national imagination so dependent on the voice of power it never thinks to question the very legitima-*

> *cy of the narrative itself and, hence, the truth as presented by a single*
> *individual.* (181. Italics mine.)

In her insightful analysis of *Jazz*'s concluding pages, Heinze asserts that
Morrison "devolv[es] upon the reader the responsibility for his or her
own vision" (181). In closing her narrative, *Jazz*'s narrator faults herself for a failure of imagination, for misperceiving characters' motives
and inaccurately predicting their behavior. After seducing readers with
a paragraph that eroticizes both the physical reader/text relationship
("the way you hold me . . . your fingers . . . turning [pages]") and the
dialogic connection with the reader that the text establishes ("Talking to
you and hearing you answer—that's the kick"), she envisions herself as
the text and literally places herself in the reader's hands in the final sentences: "Look where your hands are. Now" (229).

Morrison's word choice in the penultimate line is significant.
Throughout the novel, in his literal and metaphorical search for Wild,
Joe has been trying to place himself in her hands, or at least to get her
to extend from her hiding place a hand that would indicate to him her
acknowledgment of him as her son. Wild refuses—or is unable to comprehend or respond to his request. In the closing lines, Morrison places
the text in the role of the mother who finally, with her last breath,
acknowledges the child/reader. This mother/child figurative relationship is not, however, what we might call a "matronizing" one. In
addressing the predicament of the narrator and the writer, the narrator
stresses that her characters, like children, forge identities of their own,
beyond any that her limited imagination (or a parent's vision of what the
child will become) can construct:

> I thought I knew them and wasn't worried that they didn't really know
> about me . . . . [W]hen I invented stories about them—and doing it
> seemed so fine—I was completely in their hands . . . . all the while
> they were watching me . . . . So I missed it altogether. I was sure one
> would kill the other. I waited so I could describe it. I was so sure it
> would happen. That the past was an abused record with no choice but
> to repeat itself . . . . [T]hey were busy being original, complicated,
> changeable—human, I guess you'd say, while I was the predictable
> one, confused in my solitude into arrogance, thinking my space, my
> view was the only one that mattered. (221)

Again, Morrison undermines the idea of a narrative with a single vision of the truth, and, by extension, of a single, privileged version of history. Characters are portrayed as asserting subjectivity; they take on a life separate from that which the author has breathed into them. The narrator's assessment of the situation may be read as a metaphor for power relations in Morrison's fiction. We are imprinted with culturally constructed identities, and we resist, we revise, establishing agency, subjectivity, and identity in the process. This is not, however, a simple or linear process. Characters such as Wild and Golden Gray stand as stark reminders of the potential for falling through the structures we attempt to engage.

Jazz's upbeat conclusion stresses the fluidity of the process of identity construction and the necessary role of interactive agency in the processing of lived and historical experience. Agency—and positive male-female relations—are recoverable, *Jazz* argues. Morrison's vision of agency interrogates a liberal humanist conception of agency. In the early chapters of *Jazz*, Morrison's characters are similar to Bob Dubois in *Continental Drift*: they are ineffectual agents who fail to comprehend the social and economic currents that construct them as subjects. As the narrative develops, they develop the imagination that frees them to act as agents in the reconstruction of the self.

Jazz's characters resist the seductive draw of materialism that lures Bob Dubois to Florida and results in his penury and violent death. In Morrison's fictional world, resistance to materialism is a necessary step to the recovery of agency and identity. Violet asserts, "Before I came North I made sense and so did the world. We didn't have nothing but we didn't miss it" (207). Violet is not owning up to the whole truth of her Southern experience. She is erasing the dire poverty, the hunger and the violent racism. What cancels out all of these powerful negatives for Violet is the sense of community that she felt in the South. An interviewer reports that Morrison's mother "never once went back South to visit because her experience of it had been so bad"; however, according to Morrison "she talked about it as though it were heaven, absolute heaven" ("All that Jazz" 284). Violet sweetens the past in a similar manner.

Felice functions to reconnect Violet and Joe to a community and to guide them through a self-recovery process in which they recognize that the demons that torment them (Golden Gray and Wild) figure not only in their personal histories of oppression and resistance but also in historical narratives that shape power relations on a larger social scale. In making this connection, Violet and Joe are interactive agents working within social structures that Bob Dubois never becomes aware of. For Joe and Violet, recovering the self is an act of resistance that would not be possible outside of the context of community. Early in the novel, when Joe shoots Dorcas and Violet stabs the corpse, they are acting as autonomous agents. Their negative acts are directed at a representation of what they lack and despise rather than at the social structure as that have been instrumental in the construction of the lack. Near the close of the narrative, Violet rejects her desire to be "[w]hite[,] [l]ight[, and] [y]oung again" (208) in naming it and describing it in the past tense. Violet is able to place her misdirected act of resistance (stabbing Dorcas's corpse) in the context of a larger political economy: "What's the world for if you can't make it up the way you want it?" (208). She comprehends that it is the social structure that needs to be remade, not her body. Morrison suggests that the exercise of interpersonal, interactive agency is integral to resistance strategy. Banks concludes *Continental Drift* with the same suggestion, but his characters, with the possible exception of Vanise, fail to gain access to the resistance strategies his text privileges. Both novels are dissenting fictions: they indict and illuminate oppressive social structures, and they suggest strategies of resistance. *Continental Drift* points out the failure of individual agency as a strategy of resistance and suggests the necessity of an awareness of the subject's place within socioeconomic structures. *Jazz* situates those structures historically and emphasizes the resistance possibilities inherent in interactive agency. In this and the previous chapter, my emphasis has been on thematic concerns. The next chapter examines David Bradley's weaving of a resistance narrative into the style and structure of his fiction.

Notes

1. The term "social structures," as I use it here and throughout this study, refers primarily to the social constructs race, class, and gender.

2. Roberta Rubenstein provides a succinct analysis of the role of community in Morrison's fiction and the representation of divisions within Morrison's black communities. Susan Willis treats the effect of the Great Migration from rural South to urban North and the accompanying transition to wage labor on Morrison's fictional communities. Carolyn Denard addresses the representation of the tension between feminism and ethnicity in Morrison's work and the significance of that tension in her vision of community. Harry Reed discusses the role of Black Cultural Nationalism in "regenerat[ing] the community from within" in Morrison's work (52). Anne Bradford Warner, Elizabeth B. House, and Barbara Christian also address the constitution of community in Morrison's works.

3. See Susan Willis, "I Shop Therefore I Am," for an extended analysis of Hagar's shopping death.

4. Less dramatic examples of identity formation in response to an absent presence can be found throughout Morrison's oeuvre. Nel, in *Sula*, undergoes a transformation after her first and only meeting with her maternal grandmother, whom she later remembers only as "the woman in the canary-yellow dress" who smelled of gardenias and looked too young to be her mother's mother (25). Soon after their meeting, Nel rises from her bed at night and walks to an archetypal mirror, where she realizes for the first time, "I'm me" (28). The woman in the canary-yellow dress resurfaces as a trope for the mythical presence of Mother Africa in *Tar Baby*. Jadine catches a fleeting glance of her in a Paris marketplace. She returns the glance and spits contemptuously on the ground. Jadine is overcome with emotions that recur with frequent memories of "that woman's woman—that mother/sister/she; that unphotographable beauty" (39). Although the two never meet again, the memories destabilize Jadine's sense of

self, making her feel "lonely and inauthentic" (40). In *Paradise*, a mythical figure leads the founding families west into uncharted territory. He reappears to characters struggling with the constraints of community generations later.

5.   In *The Bluest Eye*, for example, Cholly's search for his father leads to rejection by his father, symbolic rebirth into a "dangerous freedom," and consequent inability to be a father to his children. In *Song of Solomon*, Milkman's quest uncovers a matriarchal presence: Sing.

6.   *The Bluest Eye* delves into the effects of the Great Migration on individual and family lives. Both history and the present weigh heavily on the Breedloves. They have become unmoored from community, and find individual agency inadequate against the oppression of daily lived experience. The Great Migration and the need for a connectedness with the past are addressed in *Song of Solomon* as well.

7.   Violet's mother becomes increasingly emotionally absent as her family's economic situation worsens, finally retreating into silence, and then committing suicide. Alice remembers her mother as a stern presence whose primary parenting activity was the suppression of Alice's sexuality.

8.   The history of slavery and the family tree it distorts are symbolized by the "tree" on Sethe's back in *Beloved*. Pilate is born without a navel in *Song of Solomon*. This anomaly signifies both her power and her family's being dispossessed of the land that nurtured them. Eva Peace, sacrifices her leg to support her family in *Sula*. Cholly's rage at his father and at his own economic powerlessness, and his nostalgia for the rural southern past result in his violation of his daughter's body in *The Bluest Eye*.

9.   Plum, in *Sula*, is perhaps the most memorable embodiment of the association of the desire to return to the womb with a surrender of consciousness or death wish. Eva understands that he desires to return to her womb, and she immolates him in an act she perceives as merciful.

10. Ann Hulbert also faults Morrison for creating an uncertain and unstable narrative voice.

CHAPTER 4

Identity, Masculinity, and Desire in David Bradley's Fiction

The quest for individual (or collective) manhood . . .
closely linked to the related devotionals of muscular
nationalism, racial chauvinism and sexual status
through consumerism . . . has eclipsed Christianity as
an ontology for directing our activity and orienting it
toward a coherent, ultimate goal.

—Paul Hoch *White Hero, Black Beast*

Despite recent proclamations of the death of the subject, the masculine subject in search of his manhood remains a staple of late twentieth-century narratives and cultural mythology. The elements transformed by dissenting fictions include the where, how, and if of his finding it, and the notion that manhood is a stable category. David Bradley's two novels, *South Street* (1975), and *The Chaneysville Incident* (1981) ask what it means to be a Real Man, and how race and class influence the cultural construction of maleness. Bradley's novels focus primarily on gendered identity and its relationship to resistance strategy. Like Banks's Bob Dubois, Bradley's characters struggle with the limits of individual agency. Like Toni Morrison's characters, Bradley's protagonists move beyond a liberal humanist notion of agency as they become involved in the business of recovering resistance history.

In shaping a maleness they can live with, Bradley's protagonists create woman-free zones (a Philadelphia tenement in South Street, a rural shack in *The Chaneysville Incident*). They enter these zones with a bottle of whiskey and a quixotic blueprint for maleness, provided by a male guide figure who differs only in a few minor particulars from the first novel to the second. But the quixotic grid proves a bad fit when laid down upon the lives of Bradley's late twentieth-century heterosexual protagonists. The women whom they very much wish to bed, ignore, and be alienated from (in that order), persist in creeping in from the margins and directing the quest for male identity.

Both of Bradley's novels move toward a critical point at which female desire becomes the primary engine orchestrating the action. As in Morrison's *Jazz*, female figures who represent specific moments in the history of African-American resistance to racist oppression—and who are intitially absent presences in the novels—become more present as the narrative task of reconstructing identity (in *South Street*) and history (in *Chaneysville*) progresses.

A conception of desire akin to that described by Hélène Cixous as a desire "that does not entail conflict or destruction," that does not stage "the movement toward the other . . . in a patriarchal production" is central to Bradley's work ("Sorties" 79). Female desire and the female experience of pleasure give *South Street*—an African-American male *küntslerroman*—its structure, its substance, and its plot. *South Street* at first tentatively addresses and finally embraces a libidinal economy surprisingly similar to that described by Cixous: a pleasure in being outside the self and consciously engineering its refashioning.[1] *The Chaneysville Incident* approaches its subject self-consciously and self-reflexively. It very carefully constructs a narrative about very carefully constructing a gendered identity and a patrifocal family history—until its final segments, when a feminine, oral, imaginative vision of history asserts itself as the only process through which its protagonist might resolve his dilemma.[2] Although French feminist psychoanalytic critics are rarely mentioned in the context of African-American literature, and Cixous and Bradley address disparate concerns, contexts, and cultures in their works, Cixous's writings elucidate some important elements of Bradley's works, the very elements challenged by Bradley's feminist critics: issues of gender and desire.[3] Cixous's writings do not, however, focus on the primary gender issue that concerns Bradley: the making of masculinity and the masculine identity quest. This chapter deploys contemporary theories of masculinity in the exploration of Bradley's construction of maleness and employs Cixous's work to frame a discussion of gendered desire and its relationship to identity, agency, resistance, and, in *The Chaneysville Incident*, the recovery of history. Bradley's two novels engage in a complex, fluid mode of storytelling that draws on African-American oral tradition. Like *Almanac of the Dead* (see chapter five), Bradley's works refuse an "industrial" sense of narrative time that flows from a beginning to a middle to closure. His works emphasize orality and focus on the body and sexuality as sites of resistance to culturally produced notions of gender, race, and class. In taking the conscious refashioning of gender as his subject, and in employing female characters as the primary analysts of the gendered self and the primary catalysts in its reinvention, Bradley does some important cultural work—work that has been largely overlooked by critics, who have ignored *South Street* and have focused primarily on the treatment of African-American history in *The Chaneysville Incident*.

Mainstream white America employs black maleness as a marker for its fear, rage, and ambivalence about the future. As Ishmael Reed argues, with diligent documentation, in *Airing Dirty Laundry*, the pathologizing of black maleness in the media and by social critics has reached epic proportions. Reed argues that white Americans have been quick to hold up black men's shortcomings for public scrutiny and to call for "black leadership" and slow to air the dirty laundry of their own ethnic groups or "underclass." A body of complex creative work that responds to this scapegoating with a nuanced exploration of black masculinity and black and interracial male/female power relations, Bradley's fiction has been undervalued as cultural critique. Sadly, it may be *because of* its exploration of black maleness that Bradley's work has not received the consideration it deserves. The nuanced literary exploration of black maleness has met with something less than enthusiasm in a culture that has been spoon-fed on sound bites and news clips that depict black men as armed, dangerous, and unknowable. Critics have too often confused Bradley with the male protagonists of his novels, overlooking his interrogation of the motives and methods of his characters.

This chapter addresses the notion of the gendered text, tracing the evolution, in Bradley's novels, from a masculine to a feminine mode of imaginative writing. The chapter is divided into three sections. The first reads *South Street*, the second reads *The Chaneysville Incident*, and the third addresses identity formation as resistance strategy in Bradley's work as a whole.

South Street is situated within the confines of a few blocks of South-Central Philadelphia, in the early nineteen-seventies. Its characters are working-class and unemployed prostitutes, hustlers, henchmen, bartenders, preachers, winos, and janitors. The only white folks to appear are lost and locked securely in their automobiles. *South Street* is a celebration of vernacular culture. The narrative pulses with signifying, sounding, and dozens-playing, most of it focused on female sexuality and desire.[4] Sharp-witted insult-trading, barroom declamation contests, and toasts make up the majority of the dialogue. There are declamations and toasts appealing to male fears of impotence and sexual inadequacy. Notably absent or near-absent are male declamations of larger-than-life potency, penis-size, or ability to maintain an erection.

Female bodies are constructed largely around ferocious sexual desire or terrifying sexual desirability. Big Betsy the Whore, a prostitute forced into retirement by age, is described as a warship cruising for young male flesh. Sister Fundidia, the cipher, is blind to her own larger than life sexuality, and seems to exist in the novel primarily as a life-support system for a pair of breasts said to resemble "bouncing . . . chocolate volleyballs" (281). Leslie, vulnerable on the inside, with a veneer of bitchy manipulativeness, possesses a legendary sexual appetite that lays two men low and drives one to the depths of despair. Vanessa is a prostitute paid by her pimp not to work. Female desire is initially filtered, in *South Street*, through a haze of male fear and insecurity. Male bodies are often asexual or sexually inadequate, consumed with eating and excreting, sucking alcohol directly from the bottle, chewing sandwiches, and giving vent to comic explosions in bathrooms with paper-thin walls.

Into this vernacular culture of the working-class unemployed enters Adlai Stevenson Brown, a middle-class Ivy League-educated poet who has come to seek his identity among the proletariat. Brown has just left his lover, Alicia, a black prototype of *The Chaneysville Incident*'s upper-class white intellectual, Judith. The move from penthouse to tenement is the crucial first step in Brown's identity quest. In order to explore and refashion masculine identity, Bradley removes Brown from the middle-class, integrated setting that has thus far been the backdrop for his life, emphasizing the fact that, unlike South Street's more permanent residents, members of the middle and upper classes have the option of slumming, of repositioning themselves within class structures. In moving from the class into which he was apparently born to the world of South Street, in which he is viewed with suspicion as an outsider, Brown temporarily disengages from the stability of occupying one's "assigned" position in a class hierarchy, creating a space in which identity, and identity politics, may be productively explored. Ultimately, Brown chooses something much closer to American individualism than identity politics. Bradley does not, however, endorse a liberal humanist notion of individual agency. His protagonists cling to the belief that they act as individuals, and that their actions take place outside of social structures, as does Bob Dubois in *Continental Drift.* In the final segments of both of Bradley's novels, when individual agency proves untenable, his characters come to an understanding of interpersonal agency and of the possibility of exercising it within social structures—as dissenting subjects.

Bell hooks writes that although rigid, monolithic notions of masculinity exist outside of white and integrated communities "racial integration has had a profound impact on black gender roles. It has helped to promote a climate wherein most black women and men accept sexist notions of gender roles" (hooks, *Black Looks* 93). Bradley explores masculinity, in *South Street,* outside of the sphere of direct white influence. Race, however, is still a factor in his protagonist's self-interrogation and refashioning.

Down among the proletariat, blackness is blacker and men and women are (to borrow from *Jazz*'s narrator) more "original, complicated, changeable—human" (*Jazz* 220). In Alicia's penthouse, Brown must constantly discuss, defend, and define being black, and he approaches all of these tasks in terms of class. He drinks too much, Alicia notes, and he does it without class. He says "fuck" too much. He doesn't bathe as often as he should. He doesn't act nice "'up there to the big house wid Massa,'" as he puts it, when Alicia takes him out networking among white poetry editors (53). Exasperated with Brown's definition of blackness, a definition that excludes what Brown calls her "'million-dollar Westchester County black middle-class ass,'" Alicia insists, "'I'm just as black as you are'" (52, 53). "'That,'" says Brown, "'is what frightens me'" (53). The fear of what happens to blackness when it gains middle-class respectability is what sends Brown down among the folk on South Street.

Brown's contempt for Alicia and her successful friends among the intelligentsia is apparently shared by Bradley. Characterization in this novel is drawn almost entirely along class lines, and across racial divisions. The family of Italian-American restaurateurs that occupies South Street's margins is more down-home and complicated than anyone in Alicia's elite crowd. From the brief glimpse we get of the black male intelligentsia, it appears to be constructed from the same model as the lost white man who bumbles into a bar in the opening pages, cannot speak or interpret working-class Ebonics, and ends up backing out of the door, confused, ignorant, and threatened.[5] The higher one's level of education and material success, it seems, the whiter one becomes. In Brown's schema of identity, class initially displaces race. Gender goes unexplored until Vanessa, an ex-prostitute, installs herself in his South Street walk-up and he learns that racial commonalities do not efface gender and class differences. Vanessa sees Brown as a college boy who can afford the luxury of slumming rather than as a brother. Bradley uses her to point out that Brown's sojourn on South Street is a social experiment that he can end at any time he wishes. To the Street's residents, the cultural milieu that Brown explores is a confining set of overlapping social structures from which there is no escape.

The models for maleness that Brown encounters on South Street are curiously asexual or sexually inadequate. They bring into question what bell hooks calls the "phallocentric model" for masculinity, in which "what the male does with his penis" represents the primary and most "accessible way to assert masculine status" (*Black Looks* 94).[6] Leo the Bartender's primary relationship is to food. Rayburn, Leslie's jilted husband, is unable to maintain an erection. Brother Fletcher, the Storefront preacher, gingerly holds hands with his wife in bed. He represents an alternative masculinity that is gentle, caring, playful, and selfless.

Alternative forms of gender expression are an integral component of dissenting fictions. Toni Morrison—and David Bradley—draw on alternatives to rigid gender binaries in African-American communities. Bell hooks addresses this potential for resistance:

> Throughout black male history in the United States there have been black men who were not at all interested in the patriarchal ideal. In the black community of my childhood, there was no monolithic stan-

dard of black masculinity. Though the patriarchal ideal was the most esteemed version of manhood, it was not the only version . . . . [There] were black men who chose alternative lifestyles, who questioned the *status quo*, who shunned a ready made patriarchal identity and invented themselves. (*Black Looks* 88)

Leroy Briggs aspires to a masculine model with a long history in African-American fiction: the Bad Nigger, a legendary, traditionally male figure whose cultural production responds directly to white society's fear of those it oppresses.[7] The Bad Nigger presents a fearless and frightening image of black maleness, turning the white-produced stereotype of the dishonest, violent, oversexed, brutish black man back upon its inventors. Leroy owns a numbers operation, a gambling parlor, and nearly everything else illicit and profitable on South Street. He beats his lover, Leslie, who considers the bruises signs of affection. Sexually, however, he is bested by Leslie, whose legendary sexual desire causes him, at times, to hide out in the rooms of his bodyguards lest she discover that he is on the premises and available for sexual duty. Here, as elsewhere in the novel, would-be quixotic elements of the plot are destabilized by female desire. Traditionally, the Bad Nigger is vested with legendary sexual prowess. Bradley's version of this figure, however, is less a potent trickster than an insecure minor-league crook who, had he been white, would have become a moderately successful entrepreneur. Instead, he has become a moderately successful bully and low-level crime-boss. Missing from this portrayal are the Bad Nigger's spontaneous wit and renowned sexual appetite and skill. It is his woman's desire that is legendary, and his inability to keep her satisfied destabilizes his Quixotic self-image.

Sifting among the models for definition of his caste and masculinity, Brown befriends Jake, an aging homeless wino who readily imparts cautionary advice on heterosexual relationships and what it means to be a man. The Jake blueprint for Real Maleness involves two components: avoiding contact with women, and drinking copious quantities of alcohol. Women, according to Jake, are unfathomable. "'There ain't nobody that knows nothin' 'bout women. Not even women. '*Specially* not women'" (238). Jake does know, however, that women are dangerous, that "'women's been the downfall of many a good wino'" (235). "'There's more niggers died climbin' onto some damn woman than ever died just sippin a little wine.'" Sexual contact with women, Jake cautions, will result in either the discovery of male impotency or premature ejaculation. For other men, that is. In one of the novel's few instances of male sexual braggadocio, Jake asserts

> I've got women hangin' over me all the damn time. I just ain't after it no more. Women's too damn much trouble. I'll take me a bottle a red wine any time. It keeps you warmer, it don't keep on after you if you don't want no more, it don't wake y'up in the middle a the goddamn night an' it don't never complain if you roll over an' goes to sleep soon as you're done with it.(236)

Again, the quixotic is destabilized by fear of female desire. What begins as sexual boasting concludes with a thinly veiled acknowledgment of Jake's fear of female sexuality, and the link between his fear and his alcoholism.

It is the way that Jake lives his life, rather than his cautionary advice, that Brown internalizes in his identity quest. Like many characters in dissenting fictions, Jake has parted company with the white world and its material comforts and possessions. Although it has taken place over the course of a number of years, Jake's break with middle-class materialism parallels Brown's move to South Street. Occupying the black space outside of white culture's production of identity—and paradoxically fulfilling its worst prejudices, Jake exemplifies a blackness that Brown aspires to. Jake's actions are community-oriented. He is generous, thoughtful, and honest. He shares his secretly stashed emergency bottle of wine with a fellow wino in need. It is his only possession. He brings about the removal of the community's most insincere and exploitative resident, the preacher, Rev. Sloan. Jake understands the entitlements, privileges, and constraints of class, in human terms:

> They don't call you a wino until you gets old an' smells bad and sleeps in alleys. If you live in a room someplace, then you're just a common drunk, an' if you're young and lives in an apartment, why then you're a heavy drinker. . . . An' if you're white, you gets to be an alcoholic, an if you're white an' rich an' you live someplace like Bryn Mawr, then you ain't an alcoholic, you're a national problem. (235)

In cataloguing for Brown the things one has to give up to be a successful wino, Jake catalogues the privileges of class, and he perceives them as constraints as well as privileges: "'You got to give up bein'—reglar. Can't be worryin' 'bout no clothes. Can't be worryin' 'bout no car. Can't get uptight 'bout no house, or no job. Can't be too worried 'bout food. An women—no women'" (235). Jake realizes that, as Kenneth Clatterbaugh puts it in his exploration of contemporary masculinities,

> the white patriarchal gender ideals that are held out to black men in a racist society create double binds: . . . The message to black men from patriarchy is to 'be a man'; the message from capitalism is 'no chance'. (142-43)

Brown has relocated to South Street precisely to extract himself from the privileges and constraints of class that Jake catalogues, and to explore the culturally produced relationship between race and class. Brown's decision to live the proletarian life is an act of resistance to the middle-class notion that equates a move up in social class with racial uplift. He tells Alicia, when she implores him to return to his former middle-class life,

> We all live here [on South Street]. . . . And all the carpets and college degrees in the world won't do anything but help you forget. . . . That's the one big difference between white folks and black folks: black folks never get to forget. (124)

Most of the novel's male characters subscribe, if covertly, to Jake's anti-materialist pro-brotherhood code. Those who don't, like the Reverend Sloan, are plainly the villains. Bradley asks a great deal of his working class characters when he demands that they scrutinize the allure of material success, but he is appealing to an African-American cultural and literary tradition that privileges the well-being of the community over the material accomplishments of its individual members. This tradition and its current status have been the focus of considerable attention in recent years. Haki Madhubuti sums up some of the concerns of contemporary social and cultural critics, in *Black Men*, when he writes that the lure of materialism is a major, if not the major threat to

black manhood in the U. S. today. He suggests that a stable, well-bal-
anced black masculinity and rampant consumerism cannot coexist. His
statement is equally true, I would argue, without the qualifier "black."
Madhubuti and others see troubled young black men not as nihilistic or
rebellious, as the white media portrays them, but as the products of a
blind allegiance to a capitalist system that produces young white
empire-builders like Michael Milken and Microsoft founder Bill Gates.
The situation that Malcolm X described three decades ago still exists:
"All of us—who might have probed space or cured cancer or built
industries—were, instead, black victims of the white man's American
social system," streetsmart hustlers building the only sort of empires a
racist society allowed them access to (*The Autobiography of Malcolm
X*, 90). Madhubuti argues for a masculinity focussed on improved gender relations and defined by creative extended family-building rather
than by material wealth. In his prescription for reconstructing black
heterosexual manhood, Madhubuti writes that "the root, as well as the
quality, of Black life is in the relationship established between Black
men and women in a white supremacist system. Black struggle, that is
the liberation of our people, starts in the home" (60). Bradley's characters ignore this advice, to their peril. Most of the male characters have
resisted the lure of materialism, and those who haven't are portrayed as
buffoons. They all subscribe, however, to Jake's "no women" dictum,
which sounds curiously similar to Daniel Patrick Moynihan's infamous
1965 report to the U. S. Congress on "The Negro Family," in which he
blamed black women for what he decried as the desperate state of black
manhood:

> Given the strains of the disorganized and matrifocal family life in
> which so many Negro youth come of age, the Armed Forces are a dra-
> matic and desperately needed change: a world away from women, a
> world run by strong men of unquestioned authority. (Rainwater and
> Yancey 88)

The idea of a "world away from women," a woman-free zone, is
appealing to Jake, Brown, Leo, and other characters seeking to heal bat-
tered or beleaguered masculinity. Masculinity is not equated, in
Bradley's fictional world, with the conquest of women. It is not equated with the conquest of things. It cannot be measured by the standard

yardsticks by which late capitalism defines it: "the length of one's penis, the number of one's conquests, or the size of one's bank account" (Hoch 98). Just as Jake's fear of female desire is linked to his alcoholism, fear of female sexuality and of their own inadequacy in relationships with women influences the actions of other characters in similarly negative ways. Rayburn and Leroy define themselves in terms of their ability to bring about female orgasm. Both characters interpret female desire and pleasure as currency, with the accreditation of masculinity as the payoff of the transaction.

In a scene that functions as the novel's climactic moment on many levels, Vanessa, the world-weary ex-prostitute who has moved into Brown's apartment, and Brown experience mutual orgasm, and it literally saves Brown's life. Leroy is lurking in the hall with a gun, intending to kill Brown, but when he realizes what has transpired in the bedroom, he slinks away and closets himself in his rooms to contemplate retirement. As a subscriber to the masculinity-equals-the-conquest-of-female-desire school, Leroy believes that Brown has succeeded where he failed. Again, female desire and pleasure are reified. The novel interrogates this view, albeit inconclusively. Although the reification of female pleasure is a thread running throughout the narrative, Brown seeks to understand masculinity not merely as the ability to produce female pleasure, but through an understanding of female desire. He is the first man in Vanessa's experience to understand even the basic fact that her body might be viewed as something other than a commodity. He establishes a relationship with Vanessa as he develops an understanding of her struggle as a black women in a white supremacist system, an understanding that is new to him.

It is not man's skill as a modern warrior, nor his sexual conquests, nor his material wealth that defines "real" maleness in this novel, it is his ability to produce female pleasure and to decipher female desire. Female pleasure is co-opted into the definition of masculinity, but it escapes to take center stage in *South Street*. The sexual desire of the two sisters, Vanessa and Leslie, literally controls *South Street's* action. But it is not a boisterous, playful, quixotic desire. It is a desire born of tragedy and desperation, of missed opportunities and opportunities that were never there in the first place. Leslie's sexuality is legendary and larger than life because it is the only component of her identity that has been allowed free expression. She uses it as a commodity to barter for better living conditions and a measure of the only sort of power available to her.

Cixous addresses male co-optation of female desire, and its subversion by women, throughout her theoretical work.[8] Her insistence that woman must reclaim desire and pleasure, must "signif[y] with her body" ("Laugh" 251) has been misread as essentialist, although she opens her most well known essay with a "refus[al] to confuse the biological and the cultural" ("Laugh" 245). Just as Vanessa reminds Brown that for him poverty is an "experiment," while for everyone else on *South Street* it is an existence, she subverts his attempts to co-opt female desire as a marker of masculinity. When he reminds her during an argument that he has "produced" the sexual pleasure she desired, she responds,

> "An' don't that make your ass proud. Makes you the best cock-smith on South Street. You gonna be a fuckin' legend, Brown. 'You can write it yourself, you'd like that. You go on up there an' do that, Brown, now that you finished your goddamn research. "(326)

In the sexually charged signifying that makes up most of their exchanges, Vanessa continually reminds Brown of his status as Other, and outsider, and she subverts his attempts to set up a hierarchical relationship.

Bradley's convincing portrayal of Vanessa as an intelligent, emotionally scarred, insecure, and defensive woman who has taken up prostitution in order to escape her abusive father's household, and whose sexual dis-ease is the result of male abuse and commodification, deconstructs Jake's "no-women" formula for class-consciousness. Having experienced the feminization of poverty firsthand, and having "given up" all of the things Jake deems it necessary to do without (a home, a job, a car, a "regular," ordered life), left with nothing but her body from which to make a living, Vanessa is acutely, painfully class-conscious. She seeks to place her desire and pleasure outside of the cultural milieu that commodifies it. From the moment when she installs herself in Brown's apartment, his understanding of what constitutes class becomes intimately tied to Vanessa's experience as a black woman who came to maturity on South Street. He begins to understand what

Vanessa knows all too well: that race, class and gender are intimately intertwined. Banks's Bob Dubois's tragedy is that he never achieves this understanding. Morrison's characters arrive at it through struggle. Vanessa's story exemplifies a crucial component of *écriture féminine*: it "return[s]," as Cixous puts it, "to the body which has been more than confiscated from her, which has been turned into the uncanny stranger on display—the ailing or dead figure, which so often turns out to be the nasty companion, the cause and location of inhibitions" ("Laugh" 250). Vanessa's body is both the cause and the locus of her inhibited pleasure response, and her quest for sexual pleasure is a quest to reclaim her body from the same commodity culture that Brown resists in his identity quest and Jake defines in his cataloguing of the privileges and constraints of class.

Brown's quest for identity ends, in characteristically late twentieth-century form, inconclusively. He boards a city bus, pocketing an invitation to an intelligentsia gathering at Alicia's. The passengers on the bus mirror critical components of his identity. A woman clutches her purse when he moves by her toward a seat, reacting not to Brown but to the image of black maleness in her white American imagination. He takes a seat near a well-dressed acquaintance from his days among the literati, Earl, who peruses the *New York Times Book Review*, quotes Tennyson, and admonishes Brown for abandoning "'a foxy woman, a fancy pad, a bad car. . . . You must be the craziest thing since that black astronaut thought they was gonna send him to the moon'" (337). In a comment that sounds strikingly like one of Bob Dubois's internal monologues, Earl concludes that Brown must have "'himself some stuff down there [on South Street], that's why he's there all the time. Pokin' himself some real jungle fire" (337). Earl both embodies what Brown fears he would become if he embraced the upward-mobility track and describes precisely the identity that patriarchal culture has affixed to Vanessa: "stuff," sexual goods, packaged in a black woman's body, "jungle fire."

Obviously agitated, Brown forces the bus driver to make an unscheduled stop on the South Street Bridge, the point of demarcation between South Street and the white world outside its borders. Brown steps out, and the reader is left with an image of him on the bridge, between two worlds and acutely aware of their differences—a conclusion as American as Huck Finn's lighting out for the territory or the Invisible Man's vacillation between hibernation and emergence.

Bradley's open-ended conclusion and his skillful intertwining of bawdy comic vignettes and tragic personal histories destabilize quixotic elements of the plot. Throughout *South Street*, social constructions of gender and race are introduced and parodied through the medium of ritualized vernacular insult-trading, and contested by the characters' actions and their incisive analyses of their social and physical environments. The barroom chatter centering on female desire and male inadequacy echoes the primary engine driving the plot. The identity quest motif draws its energy not from the quixotic masculine desire suggested by the comic surface plot, but from an underlying conception of desire akin to that described by Cixous—a desire "that does not entail conflict or destruction," that does not stage "the movement toward the other . . . in a patriarchal production" ("Sorties" 79). The female desire affixed to Vanessa—a desire to reclaim her body from the patriarchal capitalism that has commodified it as "jungle fire" and profited from its sale, both historically and at present—is the driving force in the novel. Brown's movement toward the Other, be it the caste-defined Other he embraces in relocating to South Street or the caste- and gender-defined Other embodied in Vanessa, is staged by Bradley as an open-ended performance, one that emphasizes the act of moving toward the Other, rather than the closure involved in subsuming the Other.

The focus on female desire and the extensive reproduction of residually oral forms of communication in *South Street* delineate a shared territory of *écriture féminine* and African-American oral tradition, of "writing the body" and privileging the voice. The movement toward the Other, in both écriture féminine and the Afro-American oral tradition, is an act of self-definition. The contestatory vernacular braggadocio and insult-trading that make up so much of *South Street*'s dialogue posit a larger than life body as a response to the marginalization of a body politic: *South Street*'s African-American working class. Cixous's discourse on woman's libidinal economy posits a female body that resists the patriarchal gaze, that occupies a larger space than that which the patriarchal gaze is capable of imagining, a body that resists categorization and regulation, "a peripheral figure that no authority can ever subjugate" ("Laugh" 253). I am not making the claim that the oppression of women and racist oppression are equivalent or interchangeable. Cixous comes dangerously close to making this claim when she likens women to "[t]he 'Dark Continent'. . . . [B]lack . . . . Their bodies,which they haven't dared enjoy, have been colonized" ("Sorties" 68). But she tempers this flight into metaphor with stark descriptions of the Algeria of her childhood, where she observed

> "Frenchmen" at the "height" of imperialist blindness, behaving in a country that was inhabited by humans as if it were peopled by nonbeings, born-slaves. . . . I saw how the white (French) superior, plutocratic, civilized world founded its power on the repression of populations who had suddenly become "invisible" . . . . Invisible as humans. ("Sorties" 70)

Both Cixous and Bradley seek to lay bare the bones of power relations, and both return to the body and to the voice, in a symbolic but also in a very physical sense. Cixous's most well known works are manifestos claiming the act of writing as an act of resistance. This assertion has long been central to discourses of resistance in African-American and other marginalized literatures. Obviously, Cixous is not "saying the same thing" as the huge multivocal body of work that constitutes African-American literature. Her interests are international in scope. She has addressed oppression and resistance in Stalinist Russia, India, South Africa, and Cambodia. Although her writings are informed by a cultural milieu far removed from the United States and its internal race wars, her work is more widely known in the U. S. than it is in France, and she frequently visits the U.S. She is not unaware of the cultural meaning of race in America.

The act of claiming a public voice has very different meanings, however, in the African-American than in the Eurocentric feminist tradition that Cixous has (rightly or wrongly) been associated with in the U. S. In African-American writing, making one's voice heard initially signified asserting—and defending—one's humanity. Eighteenth- and nineteenth-century African-American writers were burdened with this task by the reading public. The myth that black people were genetically inferior and lower on the evolutionary scale than white people was the primary justification for slavery, and it is still deployed in the service of racism today. It was cloaked in pseudo-scientific language then, and it masquerades as scientific discourse today, in works such as Herrnstein and Murray's *The Bell Curve* (1994). Recent writings by African-

American men, such as Nathan McCall's *Makes Me Wanna Holler* (1994) and Sanyika Shakur's *Monster* (1993) are still contending with the task of asserting and defending African-American humanity. Writing the body in African-American letters today means, among other things, reclaiming the cultural body that was dispersed in the African diaspora. In mainstream Western feminism, woman's humanity is not at issue; asserting a voice means claiming power and the right to self-definition, as it has and does in many marginalized discourses. "Writing the body" has been problematized by feminists in the U. S. and elsewhere who (mis)understand it as essentialist. Cixous posits the marginalized body as a site of resistance and as a speaking subject—a strategy of resistance central to African-American literature from its emergence. The marginalized body has been employed as a signifier for the body politic throughout the history of African-American letters. David Bradley draws on this tradition.

The protagonist of *The Chaneysville Incident*, John Washington, shares more than a few of Adlai Stevenson Brown's concerns about identity and class. Bradley's second novel is set in rural Pennsylvania in the late nineteen-seventies, with spatial and temporal forays south and into the nineteenth century. *The Chaneysville Incident* is concerned with the reconstruction of John Washington's family history, and with its intersection, at several critical junctures, with the history of African-American resistance to slavery and cultural domination. Mary Helen Washington, in an early review of *The Chaneysville Incident*, noted that John Washington's version of his family history is one "in which the women are only the hinges connecting one man to his male descendants, where we only know the women's lives as they contribute to the making of another man, in which all the proud, defiant, heroic gestures are accomplished by men" (Washington 13). At the conclusion of her review, Washington concedes that she does "not know what this novel is finally trying to say about women, but it is a crucial question to be dealt with" (13). In taking up that question, I would like to emphasize the *finally* in Washington's challenge, because I believe that Bradley treats the construction of gender as he does the reconstruction of history—as a process—and we must examine the process as a whole. Bradley has been influenced by a tradition that views narrative as a process, not a linear progression toward "finally"—toward "truth" or closure.

Bradley has stated that Judith, John Washington's lover and the novel's most present female character, was a late addition, "'one of the latest structures in the whole business, and she's peripheral in this sense, that it's not about her'" ("Interview" 29). The novel is "about her" only to the extent that it is about her role in the resolution of her partner's personal conflicts with his past. Judith is a white version of *South Street*'s Alicia, the upper-class intellectual who seems to exist (in both novels) largely for the purpose of making the male protagonist's life unbearable through constant interrogation of his motives. Throughout *The Chaneysville Incident*, Judith, the psychiatrist who is always on call, implores "'I need you to share with me'" (261); "'You've never shared anything with me'" (260); "'Do you want to talk about it?'" (4). She trudges through the snow ten steps behind John, trying to help, earnest, totally absorbed in his world. It's hard to believe that back in Philadelphia she is a practicing psychiatrist with, presumably, a life of her own. The reader begins to wish that she were more peripheral to this otherwise engaging narrative; nonexistent perhaps. But Judith, like the other female characters who occupy the margins of Bradley's fiction, is peripheral in a sense other than not-central or unimportant. She is always present, albeit on the periphery of the text, influencing the way in which John sees the world and reconstructs history. Throughout most of the novel, women occupy the outer reaches of John Washington's field of vision, whether he likes it or not, and for the most part, he doesn't.

The Chaneysville Incident shares some of the concerns of what Peter Schwenger defines as "the masculine mode": an overtly male, masculine, literary mode characterized by elements of the grotesque, an obsession with the penis, and a concern with recording male experience; a fiction in which "women, when they do appear, are reflectors of masculine sexuality" (Schwenger 109). Russell Banks satirizes and critiques this mode in *Continental Drift*. Bob Dubois thinks in a masculine mode, but the Vanise segments undercut this mode, and Banks portrays the "masculine" narratives of Bob's thoughts as solipsistic and as inadequate means for understanding the world and the humans who inhabit it.

The penis does not make an appearance in *The Chaneysville Incident*. The novel is, however, concerned with recording and exploring such male experiences as the bonding that occurs between men tracking and killing animals and the experience of being lynched for courting a white woman. Not until its final chapters does *The Chaneysville Incident* begin to explore, thematically and structurally, a mode that resembles *écriture féminine*.

Early in the narrative, John outlines the blueprint for Real Maleness that has been inscribed in his psyche by Old Jack Crawley, a surrogate father figure and a rural replication of *South Street*'s Jake. Old Jack's Real Man is a self-reliant, Hemingwayesque hero. He drinks, smokes, whores, hunts, fights, and just when his foes think he's not mad any more, he strikes with his truest aim (35). Femaleness, in the early chapters, is defined primarily in negatives and by its absence. In Old Jack's model, women are either gossipy "church biddies" or artful whores. This man-made, misogynist construction of femaleness undergoes significant changes, however, as John goes about the business of retrieving his history and reconstructing his sense of self and his blueprint for maleness. As John progresses from contrived mimesis of Old Jack's Real Man to a self-created construction of maleness that takes into account both his cultural heritage and the necessity of surviving in a white academic environment, the novel's construction of female gender undergoes a parallel evolution.

John's relationship with Old Jack begins early in his childhood, on the afternoon of his father's funeral. Old Jack stumbles drunkenly into the parlor and attempts to snatch the boy away with him in order to fulfill his promise to John's father, Moses, that he would train the youth in the ways of men, lest he become the "panty-waist" that a fatherless boyhood would turn him into (34). Women, says Jack, believe there is "'always gonna be somebody to help you get through things. . . that there's gonna be a man around somewheres to haul their wagon outa the mud'" (34).

According to Old Jack's model, "'[t]here's four things a man needs'": air, water, land, and sun (40). The man who possesses all four elements, Old Jack tells John, is a satisfied animal, but if he stops at mere possession,

> he won't be a man. He won't be a man on accounta he can't make
> none a them things. So he ain't got no say. If he don't have no say
> over the things he needs to live, he ain't got no say over whether he
> lives at all, an' if he ain't got no say over that, he ain't no man. A man
> has to have say." (41)

What Old Jack appears to be getting at, in this circuitous definition by negation, is a means to power. Control over the four elements is equated with control over one's environment, which is in turn equated with control over language. Air and water are for sustenance, but earth and fire are the means of control. The land is "'a place to [make a] stand'" (40), and "'the sun is power'" (41). The destructive power of fire is especially important, throughout *The Chaneysville Incident*. Fire "'gives a man say. Gives him *final* say,'" says Old Jack. "'It lets him destroy'" (42). The Real Man then, according to Old Jack's paradigm, is a being who controls his universe through the use of force, and the correct use of force gives him control over language—"say."

Paul Hoch identifies two distinct models for masculinity that, "for the last three thousand years the manly ideal for the leading social class has oscillated sharply between":

> On the one hand a sort of hard-working, hard fighting 'puritan' hero who adheres to a production ethic of duty before pleasure; and, on the other, a more aristocratic 'playboy' who lives according to an ethic of leisure and sensual indulgence. (118)

These are precisely the masculinities that Bob Dubois is trapped between. Old Jack's model for manhood addresses elements of both puritan and playboy. Hoch points out that "not only, as in ages past, do playboy and puritan compete for dominance at the top of society, but increasingly they compete with nearly equal force for the consciousness of every man" (156). The acting out of these competing models for manhood produced by the dominant, white "top of society" Hoch refers to is nearly fatal to Bradley's black characters who exist on the margins of that society. Jack's friend Josh expresses a romantic devil-may-care playboy masculinity when he flirts with a white woman in the next county. The competing puritan component of his masculinity allows him to believe that if he presents himself as a hard-working respectable citizen, her father will give his blessing to their marriage. The fact that the white world views him primarily in terms of his race and denies/fears his masculinity complicates the situation immeasurably. Perhaps Josh is so blinded by his romantic love for the young white woman that he denies that his race matters, or perhaps he is asserting his black masculinity as a direct challenge to the white bigotry her father represents. His actions are presented as incomprehensible to his friends; his motives are never revealed. In courting the white woman, and asserting himself as her equal, perhaps Josh is simply asserting his humanity. It is a near-fatal act of resistance. He narrowly escapes being lynched, an experience that psychologically emasculates him. The lynching ritual is specifically designed to deny his humanity. The white-robed would-be lynchers, whom Jack, the town shoe-shine man, recognizes by their shoes as the pillars of the white community, make it clear that what would be a perfectly acceptable expression of masculinity in a white man is grounds for murdering a black man.

Like Moses Washington (John's father), Old Jack perceives women as a source of danger: "'Now, we know white men ain't worth dog dung, but it strikes me that any kinda woman is a mighty powerful thing to fool with'" (91). All women are constructed by Old Jack as suspect. In *South Street*'s identity schema, class displaces race; in *Chaneysville*'s schema, the category of gender initially appears to subsume that of race, and class conflicts are played out not at the center but in the margins of the narrative. In *Chaneysville*, more so than in *South Street*, these categories blur into ambiguity, as they often do in our lived experience. Both women and white people are constructed as dangerous, deceitful, and unpredictable in Old Jack's schema. There are white men, black men, and "'*any* kinda wom[e]n'" (91). "'White folks'" are "'[u]npredictable as a copperhead, an' could be the bite's poison too . . .'" (89). In the Old Jack schema, women, like white people, bite. They "'sit around takin' little bites out a [you] all day long . . .'" (37). John's mother, Yvette, who is black, falls into the same suspect category as white people. From earliest childhood, she indoctrinates her sons into subservience and silent acquiescence to white authority.

Women, in Old Jack's model, "'do more harm to a man than whiskey ever did'" (32). This assertion echoes Jake's stated preference for cheap wine over complicated women. Whiskey, young John tells Jack at their first meeting, is "'bad for you . . . . It makes you do bad things. And it makes you sick'" (32). "'You been talkin' to them Christians too much,'" Jack replies. "'Hell, boy, you could say all those things about women'" (32). Again echoing Jake, Old Jack tells John that whiskey might make a man sick, but women will kill him. Women, according to

Old Jack, are responsible for the typhus epidemic that wiped out more than half of Raystown's black community when he was a child. "'Old Jack always figured it was the women's fault,'" John tells Judith. "'They isolated disease carriers and they kept the whole thing quiet as the grave'" (273). The women kept the news of the epidemic from the white folks because they wanted to keep their jobs in the white folks' homes—the jobs that supported the entire community during the winter when the men could not find work, but Jack does not take this into account. Women, like disease, says Jack, "'make a man weak'" (69). Judith addresses the conflation of femaleness, whiteness, and disease, when, in a moment of anger, she confronts John: "'I was thinking all the time there was something wrong with you. But it's me, isn't it? I've got this horrible skin disease. I'm white'" (73).

In Old Jack's narrative of the incident at the emotional core of *The Chaneysville Incident*, in which Josh is nearly lynched for courting the white woman, Josh is imperiled because of his attraction to the white Clydette's body, and he is betrayed by her speech. In Jack's version of the story, Clydette betrays Josh to her father and his motley band of would-be lynchers by disclosing the details of their affair and the time of their next tryst. There is considerable evidence in Jack's tale to support an alternative reading, in which scanty information is beaten out of an unwilling Clydette by her father, but Jack assumes her guilt, primarily because of her race and gender. To Jack, woman's power to harm is two-fold: her body is a locus of danger and disease, and her speech can bring about a man's death. Female speech subverts and erases male control over the four elements—it abrogates masculine "say."

After Old Jack's death, John undergoes a sea change. As he prepares to bury his surrogate father, he begins to question what he knows about the life and mysterious death of his biological father, Moses. Up until this point, John has sought his identity by looking backward, tracing his male descent line, and identifying with his father, a man whose masculinity was constructed in the Real Man tradition outlined by Old Jack. The text has followed, until this point, a distinctly masculine literary tradition; a tradition based on the search for the father, be he real or metaphorical. Ellen Friedman sees this tradition as grounded in "the profoundly nostalgic conviction that the past has explanatory or redemptive powers. This belief is expressed as the futile desire to stop time or to understand, recoup, or recreate the past, summoning it into the present" (241). In its final segments, *The Chaneysville Incident* veers sharply away from the masculine yearning for the patriarchal past and enters into a tradition that Friedman associates with female-authored modern and postmodern texts: "the search for individuality, for selfhood, in the context of the cultural construction of identity" (243). Bradley's engagement with this mode indicates that the gender of the text, rather than that of its author, ought to be the primary concern of the critic investigating gendered writing. *The Chaneysville Incident* is a transgendered text: it moves from a distinctly masculine to an ambiguously feminine mode.

As he prepares to set out alone on the novel's final quest—the quest for the truth about Moses's death and his family history—John is inexplicably drawn to his mother's house, an unintended stop. Standing in the snow, looking into the darkened house, he realizes, suddenly, that

> for a dozen years she had lived with a man who was so crazy that one day he was going to walk twenty-two miles just to find a nice spot in which to blow his brains out, and so preoccupied as not only to do it, but not to care about the effect of it on his wife—and his children—to try and make it look like an accident; a man who showed her no mercy. (307)

This radical shift in perspective, in which John actually begins to see through a woman's eyes, marks a change in his attitude towards women, and a change in the novel's construction of gender. Women are no longer peripheral.

The novel addresses the process of gendered identity construction directly, in its final segments, when John reaches a dead end in his recovery of history and solicits Judith's assistance. The process of recovering history becomes analogous to the process of writing the text, and both of these merge into the process of John's reinventing his identity. This fluid exchange between theme, style, and structure exemplifies critical components of *écriture féminine*. Judith literally discovers the "story" of John's history with her body, by tripping over a grave-marker in the snow. She then imagines or intuits the story, and passes it on orally to John, who then reimagines it, conflating Judith's imagined story with the history he knows and the history he is now able to imagine. John then sits in Old Jack's chair and orally creates the text in telling the story to Judith. All of this not only becomes the text; it is recorded in the text of the novel as a process.

In the act of imagining history, John steps beyond the parameters of Old Jack's Real Man construction, and the history he finally reconstructs is dominated by an imposing and heroic female figure: his grandfather's lover, Harriette Brewer. In the closing segments of the novel, Bradley imagines history as a story. His character (Washington) first tried to access history as a text, tracking competing and conflicting narratives encoded in documents and transferring this information to his index card file. Having found this masculine mode of recovery untenable, he reconstructs history as an oral narrative, and he gains access to a usable past.

With the creation of Harriette, the novel's construction of the hero is ungendered. Harriette is a female recasting of the Real Man, minus a few of his more objectionable personal habits. The only significant difference between Harriette and Old Jack's man-who-controls-his-environment-through-the-use-of-force is that all of Harriette's actions are motivated by a desire to serve the black community. The Real Man, as personified by Moses and Old Jack, is a community servant—he steals chickens to feed the hungry, he makes hefty contributions to the church collection plate, he carries ice on his back to help a single mother nurse her fevered child through the night—but community service, although an important component of his code of honor, is not his primary motivating factor. In a reversal of traditional gendered notions of public and private, Old Jack's Real Man does not publicly acknowledge his concern for the welfare of the community; his acts are private.

John's imaginative reconstruction of Harriette is set in the 1850s. Harriette leads a desperate band of escaped slaves, with a posse of slavecatchers at their heels, on a hopeless quest for freedom. Just before dawn, surrounded by fast-approaching slavecatchers, they bravely choose death rather than surrender. One by one, they commit suicide. Harriette's is the last remaining voice, singing. Hers is the most difficult task: she is the last in the group to take her own life. She retains what Old Jack would call *final* say, and she performs what Cixous calls the act of "inscrib[ing] the breath of the whole woman" ("Laugh" 250). Cixous identifies song as the "element which never stops resonating . . . the first music from the first voice of love" ("Laugh" 251). Harriette's is the voice that ties together the loose ends of John's history. In his narrative

of Harriette's last desperate hours, John imagines men and women sharing equally the burdens and responsibilities of organized resistance. He
is unable to conclude his story, to reconcile his history and his present,
until he brings a heroic female figure in from the periphery to the center of history.

John sits down in Old Jack's cabin to tell Judith the story of Harriette
and C. K. (his grandfather), the story she has been trying to wrench
from him for years, and which he could not tell, because he had not
imagined it, until this moment. It is inarguably *his*tory, not hers, and in
this sense, Judith remains a marginal character, as do all women, pre-
Harriette, in John's recasting of history. As Bradley reminds us, however, "'it's not about her'" ("Interview" 29)—it is a story about men
narrated by a man who is attempting to come to terms with, among
other things, a rigid definition of maleness that was intentionally
inscribed upon his developing psyche during childhood by a powerful
trickster figure—and we would be imposing a feminist version of
enforced social realism if we demanded that this narrative of a male
character's re-envisioning of history in an attempt to resolve present
conflicts exhibit a more equitable gender balance. *The Chaneysville
Incident* is a novel more concerned with the construction of gender—as
a process—than with an equitable distribution of positive character
traits based on gender.

For some readers, John's rejection of old Jack's misogynist values,
in the final chapters of the novel, comes too late. Some readers find the
conclusion troubling as well. John sends Judith away so that he can
build a fire and exercise his manly control over the forces of nature in
the symbolic act of burning the artifacts that represent his former self.
Since John thinks good thoughts about Judith while he is igniting the
blaze, some critics see the ending as hopeful. Klaus Ensslen, in a
thoughtful psychoanalytic critique of the novel, even goes so far as to
call the ending "utopian" (293). But there are as many indicators that
John is contemplating suicide in the last four paragraphs as there are
symbols of unity. He "didn't bother with [packing his] things," perhaps
because he won't be needing them where he is going (431). He arranges
his father's diaries, maps, and folio, and the unused matches neatly in
their places on the cabin shelves, "ready for the next man," just as
Moses did before committing suicide (431). He twice refers to the fire
as a "pyre" (431). "A bit careless," he spills some kerosene on his boots

and remarks "but that would make no difference" (431). And finally, he stands by the pile of artifacts and "think[s] about all of it, one last time," thinking "how strange it would all look to someone else, someone from far away . . . . I wondered if that someone would understand. Not just someone; Judith . . . . I wondered if she would understand when she saw the smoke go rising from the far side of the Hill" (432).

It is possible that John's ritual to exorcise the demons from his past will include the act of self-immolation. John is, as David Bradley has stated in an interview, "'a little extreme about a lot of things . . . . This guy's crazy'" (27, 29). The feminine, imaginative reconstruction of history may be his *final* say, analogous to Harriette's singing in the face of death; what Cixous would term the inscription of his whole breath. Or the pyre may be his final say, his farewell, to his need to recoup the past. I like to think that it is the psychic remains of his father, of *the* father, that John—and Bradley—are igniting in the closing scene, as John reenters the present and looks toward the future. Just as Ellison's Invisible Man burns the contents of his briefcase—the evidence of his visibility, of his established identity—to light the darkness of the tunnel he finds himself in at the novel's close, John burns the artifacts of his identity quest. Unlike Ellison's solipsistic protagonist, however, John watches the fire and imagines connection with another human being. As in *South Street*, Bradley leaves the conclusion up to the reader. In the end, whichever ending one prefers, men and women are closer to a mutual understanding than Old Jack would have believed possible. Women occupy a central, positively charged space in John Washington's imagination. In the process of merging the structurally and thematically phallocentric story that he has assembled as a file of color-coded index cards with Judith's imaginative oral reconstruction of history, John has reinvented his history and his identity.

In both *South Street* and *The Chaneysville Incident*, female figures are the catalysts in the exploration of male identity. Cixous notes that this phenomenon, in itself, is not extraordinary. In a critique of Hegel, she points out that "the subject's going out into the other in *order to come back* to itself, this entire process . . . is, in fact, what is commonly at work in our everyday banality ("Sorties" 78). If one only fixes the Other in one's gaze in order to affirm one's sense of self, nothing out of the ordinary has taken place. Cixous continues:

... in the (Hegelian) schema of recognition, there is no place for the other, for an equal other, for a whole and living woman. She must recognize ... the male partner, and in the time it takes to do this, she must disappear, leaving him to gain Imaginary profit, to win Imaginary victory. The good woman, therefore, is the one who resists long enough for him to feel both his power over her and his desire ... and not too much, to give him the pleasure of enjoying, without too many obstacles, the return to himself which he, grown greater—reassured in his own eyes, is making. ("Sorties" 79-80)

In *The Chaneysville Incident*, Judith may be interpreted as serving the "good woman" function Cixous describes here. The "desire that does not entail conflict and destruction" ("Sorties" 79), is most successfully manifested in John's imaginative creation of Harriette Brewer.

In *South Street*, desire is embodied in Vanessa, who serves as a guide figure in Brown's exploration of masculine identities. *South Street* approaches what Cixous describes as the "*jouissance*" of "writing the body" (82).[9] The body, in *South Street*, writes the book. Bodily functions and appetites provide the substance and the subject of both the tragedy and the comedy at the center of the narrative. Female sexual and emotional desire serves as the structuring device that orchestrates the actions of male characters and propels the novel's plot. Female orgasm is the event around which *South Street*'s plot turns. Its occurrence or failure to occur decides whether Adlai Stevenson Brown will live or die, and it is the event around which male identity is decentered and reconstituted.

Bradley's fiction embodies a fluid exploration of masculine identity rather than a linear progression from the earlier text to the later. In *South Street*, class and race merge to delineate an identity politics that equates blackness with the working class and questions the value of assimilation and upward mobility. *The Chaneysville Incident* focuses on the interplay between gender and race in the fashioning of identity. Both narratives cast race as a critical component of gendered identity: *Chaneysville* in its embrace of African-American history, and *South Street* in its exploration of the relationship between class and race-based identities.

Both *South Street* and *The Chaneysville Incident* draw on what Cixous calls "the vast resources" of "feminine energy" ("Sorties" 91).

This energy is expressed in the fluid improvisational jazz mode that shapes Bradley's fiction and in its innovative exploration of the relationship between race, class, and gender.

Notes

1. Cixous describes a "woman's libidinal economy," that "takes pleasure in being boundless, outside self, outside same, far from a `center'" ("Sorties" 90, 91).

2. By "feminine" here, I refer to the qualities associated with what Cixous calls "classic representations of women[:] sensitive—intuitive—dreamy, etc." ("The Laugh of the Medusa" 248). In *The Chaneysville Incident*, the feminine mode of storytelling is also "feminine" in terms of its being introduced by and associated with female characters, until late in the novel, when it is adapted by the protagonist, John Washington.

3. Mary Helen Washington states the feminist case against Bradley succinctly. I address her concerns later in this chapter.

4. Signifying is a complex form of contestatory insult-trading, boasting, and challenging. Sounding involves more straightforward taunting and boasting. Playing the dozens involves sexually explicit insult-trading, usually directed at the auditor's mother. Bernard Bell discusses the significance of these and other residually oral forms of communication in the African-American novel in *The Afro-American Novel and Its Tradition*.

5. "Ebonics" is a term coined by black linguists that combines the words ebony and phonetics. Jerome D. Williams et al. define it as "an all-encompassing label for linguistic and paralinguistic features of the verbal and nonverbal sounds, cues, and gestures that are systematically and predictably used in the process of communication by Blacks in the United States" (638). Mary Rhodes Hoover equates it with "Black language."

6. Paul Hoch traces the evolution of the phallocentric model from an early American, production-centered economy that valorized a masculinity based on a man's ability to provide for and exert economic power over women, to late capitalism's consumer economy that valorizes a "playboy," penis-centered mas-

culinity maintained through sexual conquest. *South Street* ultimately rejects, and parodies, both of these.

   7. Bernard Bell discusses the Bad Nigger in terms of both "the white American myth of the depraved emancipated black Southerner" and a black heroic model (159). In the white American myth, "as popularized in the post-Reconstruction fiction of Thomas Nelson Page and Thomas Dixon, the Bad Nigger is bestial and criminal in nature" (Bell 159). The black heroic model subverts this myth. "Deprived of the opportunity to live free and full lives because they are black and poor, some radical black individuals who heroically defy the power of whites, ambivalently called Bad Niggers by fellow blacks, use rebellion as an act of self-affirmation" (Bell 159).

   8. Co-optation and subversion are key thematic elements in "Sorties" and "The Laugh of the Medusa."

   9. Translations of *jouissance*, which appears in French in the English translation of "Sorties," include delight, enjoyment, and sexual ecstasy.

CHAPTER 5

The Center of Power is Nothing: Storytelling, History, and Resistance in Leslie Marmon Silko's *Almanac of the Dead*

It Pleases

Far above the dome
Of the capitol—
It's true!
A large bird soars
Against white cloud,
Wings arced,
Sailing easy in this
humid, southern sun-blurred
breeze—

      the dark-suited policeman
      watches tourist cars—

And the center,
The Center of Power is nothing!
Nothing here.
Old white stone domes,
Strangely quiet people,

Earth-sky-bird patterns
      idly interlacing

The world does what it pleases.

Washington D.C. XI:73
—Gary Snyder
Turtle Island

Of all the dissenting fictions addressed in this study, Leslie Marmon Silko's *Almanac of the Dead* (1991) is the most concerned with organized resistance to oppression. The *Almanac*, an epic set in the present and near future, prophecies a Pan-American uprising of Native peoples against the neocolonialist powers that rule the Americas. Identity, for Silko, is intimately bound to a sense of place; the return of Native lands, therefore, is the primary goal of the resistance efforts that unfold in the *Almanac*. The agency that emerges in these efforts is engaged, interactive, and collective. Silko's characters act not only with an awareness of class structures, but with the goal of bringing about radical changes in those structures. The *Almanac* constructs identity as a complex interaction between place, class, ethnicity, gender, and ways of knowing and seeing. Silko portrays Native Americans, as Susan Pérez Castillo puts it, "not as Noble Savage victims or as dying representatives of a lost authenticity, but as tough, compassionate people who use the vital capacity of discourse to shape—and not merely reflect—reality" (294). Storytelling is not merely a vehicle for resistance strategy in the *Almanac*, it is an act of resistance.

This chapter explores the *Almanac*'s complex interweaving of three components of resistance strategy that will remain central in the next two chapters: the recovery of marginalized historical narratives of resistance; the explicit address of the function of discourse itself in resistance strategy, and of storytelling in particular; and the attempt to resolve the conflict between the portrayal of the body as the site of oppression and as the locus of a resisting subjectivity.

Like Morrison, Silko employs multiple perspectives in the process of recovering history. Morrison, Bradley, and Silko construct history as the lived experience of embodied resisting subjects. Their strategy for claiming history as the province of marginalized subjects involves the simultaneous decentering and foregrounding of actual historical events. Events such as the silent march down fifth Avenue, the East St. Louis riots, and the Great Migration North in *Jazz* and the colonization of the Americas in *Almanac of the Dead* are foregrounded thematically. They are decentered, however, by a focus not on the event as an occurrence with a beginning, middle, and end; a story that fits into a dominant discourse on progress and nation-building—but on the aftermath of the event, the effects of the event on the lives of marginalized subjects far removed in time and space from the actual event.

This chapter explores the means by which Silko deploys interconnected stories of intimate power relationships and a Pueblo perspective on gender to foreground class structures, to explicate power relations on a larger social scale, and to construct cross-cultural resistance strategies. In the final segment, I address Silko's strategies for introducing the body into history and into resistance strategy.

Many readers have difficulty with the *Almanac*'s narrative style and structure. There is no overarching narrative thread or "central" character. There is no clear beginning, middle, or end to its action. Rather, it is a collection of stories interwoven in a nonhierarchical fashion. By placing Silko's work within a Pueblo storytelling tradition and a cyclical rather than linear time frame, and by exploring both the influences and innovations in Silko's narrative style, I address, and—I hope—defuse the reader's anxiety.

From Silko's perspective, and from a Laguna Pueblo perspective, there is no separation of stories by type. In her essay "Language and Literature from a Pueblo Indian Perspective," Silko writes that

> anthropologists and ethnologists have, for a long time, differentiated the types of stories the Pueblo people tell. They tended to elevate the old, sacred, and traditional stories and to brush aside the family stories, the family's account of itself. But in Pueblo culture, these family stories are given equal recognition. (85)

Silko reiterates that "we make no distinctions between types of story—historical, sacred, plain gossip—because these distinctions are not useful when discussing the Pueblo *experience* of language" ("Language and Literature" 86).

Silko has said that the *Almanac* "go[es] a bit into the future," that it is both story and prophesy ("A Leslie Marmon Silko Interview" 105) The almanac referred to in the title is the Mayan almanac, which is actually four manuscripts, known collectively as the Mayan codices. According to Silko,

> [t]he almanacs were literally like a farmer's almanac. They told you the identity of the days, but not only what days were good to plant on, but some days that were extremely dangerous. There were some years that were extremely unfortunate with famine and war. There were

other years, even epochs, that would come that would be extremely glorious and fertile.   ("A Leslie Marmon Silko Interview" 104)

Silko imagines that there is a fifth manuscript, and that her characters have come into the possession of fragments of it. Additionally, the entire novel functions as a codice or prophesy. The narrative is punctuated with fragments of the Mayan manuscript. It is also clear that the revolutionary action of the novel, as well as the general atmosphere of violence and greed pervading the "epoch" in which the events unfold, is foretold in the fictional manuscript. The epoch that Silko's fictional Mayan codice foresees—an epoch that begins with the arrival of Europeans in America and lasts into the present and beyond—is the epoch of the Death-Eye Dog. According to ancient prophecy, as constructed in the *Almanac*, "During the epoch of the Death-Eye Dog, human beings, especially the alien invaders, would become obsessed with hungers and impulses commonly seen in wild dogs" (251). The epoch is characterized by greed, displacement, and blood-lust.

The *Almanac*'s deconstruction of the boundaries between story, history, and the "real" is crucial to its construction of history as a type of narrative indistinguishable from any other type. The history at the core of the *Almanac* is presented at one point within its pages in the form of the barest facts:

1500—72 million people lived in North, Central, and South America.
1600—10 million people live in North, Central, and South America. (530)

In between these two terse statements, the engines of the European conquest of America are set in motion.

For Silko, making stories is analogous to making history.   Every story has something to contribute to a larger narrative about power relations, about relationships between people and between humans and the land.   One storyteller begins, others "contribute some detail or opinion or alternative vision" (*Almanac* 224).   Thus, the poststructuralist problem of locating historical "truth," or of the impossibility of doing so, is decentered.   New interpretations and "revisionist" histories become, simply, parts of the story, a story that does "not run in a line for the horizon but circle[s] and spiral[s] like the red-tailed hawk" (*Almanac* 224).

Silko's polyvocal narrative history decenters the problem of a locatable historical truth not by avoiding it, or by replacing one truth with many truths, but by insisting that the function of story, and therefore of history, has little to do with "truth," that truth is irrelevant. From Silko's Pueblo perspective, stories have many functions: they stress the open-endedness of the narrative process; they teach proper behavior; they stress the importance of the community and foreground the interconnectedness of communities; and they provide information about geography, language, cooking, and many other concerns.[1] Their "truth," however, is not at issue. Many of these functions can be discerned in the *Almanac*'s network of stories. In stressing the interconnectedness of communities and the importance of community, the *Almanac*'s stories foreground class structures and interpersonal agency. Crossing cultural, racial, and ethnic divides that are rarely negotiated in contemporary American imaginative writing (or in contemporary resistance struggles), Silko mobilizes diverse sources of resistance, intertwining intimate, State, and global power relations. She explores the possibility of a cross-cultural coalition politics. Silko, a self-described "mixed blood," has asserted that "community is tremendously important. That's where a person's identity has to come from, not from racial blood quantum levels" ("Stories and Their Tellers" 19). Edith Swan notes that Silko's background has shaped this perspective:

> [Laguna] pueblo is located in northwestern New Mexico at the foot of Mount Taylor, a mountain sacred in traditional theology. Mixed blood predominates due to Laguna's founding, and this community is unique in this respect among the other matrilineal pueblos of the Southwest. Instead of exhibiting the common denominators of genetic and cultural homogeneity, Laguna is a proverbial melting pot, uniting diverse groups and their varying cultures. ("Feminine Perspectives at Laguna Pueblo" 309)

In the *Almanac*, Silko constructs a resistance community that includes Native American spiritual leaders, Marxist Yaqui Indians based in southern Mexico, Yupik Indians, homeless African-American and white European-American Vietnam veterans, Yaqui Indians based in Tucson, environmental activists, and a network of prison inmates across the U. S. Silko does not, however, portray this culturally diverse community as "color-blind" or conflict-free, terms in which multiculturalism is too often envisioned in contemporary discourse. They are united by their common knowledge that "the law crushed and cheated the poor whatever color they were" (*Almanac* 714). Throughout dissenting fictions, class is the critical unifying factor in resistance struggle. Nowhere is this more apparent than in the *Almanac*, which rejects simplistic notions of a universal Native American identity and pursues the idea of class-based resistance. Racial struggles are subsumed by class struggles because

> nothing could be black only or brown only or white only anymore. The ancient prophecies had foretold a time when the destruction by man had left the earth desolate, and the human race was itself endangered. This was the last chance the people had against the Destroyers, and they would never prevail if they did not work together as a common force (747).

Reviews of the *Almanac* in the mainstream press attempted to efface the class issues and the possibility of multicultural resistance movement that the novel emphasizes. They expressed a predictable discomfort with the idea of Native American uprising. Reviewers frequently employed "vengeful" as a catch-all adjective to describe the book. John Skow, for example, worried about the *Almanac*'s "very angry author," whom he described as possessing "more than a little self-righteousness." In contemporary public discourse, it seems that anger and self-righteousness are acceptable only when they are deployed by straight white middle-class men lashing out against what they see as the erosion of their privileged status. Skow's and other, similar reviews reveal more about the reviewer's (and mainstream U.S. culture's) fear and guilt than they do about the novel's actual concerns. Reviewers reduced the *Almanac*'s complex themes to issues of vengeance and retribution rather than justice. Elizabeth Tallent, reviewing the *Almanac* in the *New York Times Book Review*, fretted that Silko "equat[es] 'justice' with random violence." Tallent's phrasing is particularly revealing in its inaccuracy. Nearly all of the violence against living beings committed in the *Almanac* is committed by agents of the State, or their partners in crime, against marginalized peoples, and none of it is random. Mainstream reviewers chose to overlook the fact that the *Almanac* is as concerned with class oppression and with exploring the possibility of class as a unifying factor in resistance struggles as it is with the oppression and resistance of Native Americans. The New Right's evocation of "class warfare" in its successful attempt to silence formal opposition to its war on the poor reveals its fear of working-class unity. This is precisely the unconscious fear expressed in the reviews—fear of a broad-based working-class resistance effort. Tallent refers to the organized resistance in the *Almanac* as "a far-flung conspiracy." Skow sets up a conflict between Natives and "white society," as though the latter is a homogeneous mass that includes everyone not in the "Native" category. Silko views contemporary America in considerably more nuanced tones.

The *Almanac* makes it clear that to the resistance, "nothing mattered but taking back tribal land" (517). Their struggle is not a war of ethnic cleansing or tribal vengeance, it is a struggle to reclaim stolen land. It is a class struggle, not a race war: "battle lines will be drawn according to color: green, the color of money, the only color that had ever mattered" (406).

Indian, for Silko, is a way of knowing, a way of seeing—a cultural stance—not just a matter of lineage. Being "Indian" is not the same as looking Indian, as having Indian blood. We see this in the case of Menardo, who denies his Indian heritage and even invents a story to explain away his facial features. He reconstructs himself as so determinedly non-Indian that he sees his Indian chauffeur Tacho as the alien Other. Ironically, the chief component of character that Menardo finds so compelling in Tacho has to do with a tolerance of difference. Mainstream white identity, according to the *Almanac*'s narrator, revolves around a normalizing urge, a willful blindness to difference. This parallels Morrison's claim, in *Playing in the Dark*, that white identity, in canonical American literature, is constructed through the process of employing the difference of the Other to affirm the universality of whiteness. White Euro-Americans, however, make up an important segment of Silko's People's Army. White folks are welcome to join, if they have learned to see differently—in essence, to acknowledge and accept difference in a nonhierarchical way.

Silko weaves together a wide range of interconnected, intimate, interpersonal narratives that function to tell a story of power relations on a grand social scale and to suggest strategies of resistance. I turn

now to a close reading of two of these narrative threads that I believe
are central to Silko's argument about identity, history, and resistance:
the story of the missing baby Monte, and that of Menardo and his chauffeur Tacho.

We learn, as the narrative progresses, that Monte has been kidnapped
by his father and Beaufrey, his father's sexual partner—who is gay,
white, and the embodiment of the Reign of the Death-Eye Dog.[2] The
youth has been taken to Colombia, re-kidnapped by armed mercenaries
acting under Beaufrey's orders, and dissected for the dual purposes of
pornographic torture-video production and transplantable organ harvest, from which Beaufrey will reap dual profits.

Although Monte is barely present in the text, he has two significant
representational functions that are crucial to the *Almanac*'s perspective
on history and, therefore, to its resistance strategy. His primary function is to symbolize what we might think of as the soul of European man
after his arrival in America with the conquistadors. The reason for the
bloodlust, greed, and insanity that presently rule the American marketplace, dictate U.S. foreign relations, and pervade our culture in general,
Silko argues, is a simple one: "Europeans overseas had been alone,
without families to call them back to their senses" (*Almanac* 425). The
Europeans who colonized the Americas, and who still rule over them,
cut crucial ties to their homeland by establishing new, nationalist identities. For Silko, geography is identity. Unmoored from family and
place, "the colonial slave masters [were] suddenly . . . without their own
people and culture to help control the terrible compulsions and hungers
aroused by owning human slaves" (425). We may view young Monte
as the wandering soul—or the last in the line—of the European-
American patriarch, from the conquistadors to the Rockefellers, mired
in the perverse and violent relationship between profit and desire, and
utterly lost.

Monte's secondary function is to stress that the colonizers will be
done in by their own kind: Euro-American males. The infant is murdered with his father's unwitting complicity. A prominent theme in the
Almanac is the prophesy, common to many Native American cultures,
that the European colonizers will bring about their own end, and that the
Native resistance need only allow them to do it.

All the people had to do was be patient and wait. Five hundred years, or five lifetimes, were nothing to people who had already lived in the Americas for twenty or thirty thousand years. The prophecies said gradually all traces of Europeans in America would disappear and, at last, the people would retake the land. (*Almanac* 631-32)

Old prophets were adamant; the disappearance would not be caused by military action, necessarily, or by military action alone. The white man would someday disappear all by himself. The disappearance had already begun at the spiritual level. (*Almanac* 511)

This prophecy works in stark contrast to Euro-American biblically-inspired doomsday prophesies that link the end of Judeo-Christian patriarchy with the end of the world—the end of all life and the cataclysmic end of the planet itself. The *Almanac*'s prophesies posit the earth as permanent. Even if the white man succeeds in destroying every living thing on the planet, the narrator notes at one point, the planet itself will survive, and life will be regenerated. Monte represents the future of late capitalist patriarchy, and the prospects for its survival, as depicted in the *Almanac*, are dim. Personal quests for identity and power converge around Monte's absent presence, like the spokes of the wheel that order the map on the text's inside cover, into a massive resistance effort that will reclaim and redefine power in the Americas.

The narrative of Monte's disappearance and death is central to my analysis because it exemplifies the manner in which Silko connects local and intimate power relations and state-level power relations. The Monte narrative seems to be positioned at the local and intimate level, as a custody struggle between his parents that is intruded upon by Beaufrey for the purposes of his own perverse pleasure and profit. Beaufrey derives personal pleasure and power from Seese's agony, from the sexual stimulation he experiences when watching the dissection/murder videos, and from baiting David with feigned concern over the infant's whereabouts. He profits from the sale of the videos. Beaufrey also serves as a direct link between local and state power relations. His commerce in torture videos is partially dependent upon agents of state terror who provide him with videos of actual tortures and interrogations of prisoners, which he reproduces and sells to private collectors who use them to achieve private pleasures. Silko deploys the

Monte narrative, then, to connect intimate and global power relations, and to suggest that resistance at the local level where power asserts itself, be it the body, the intimate relationship, or the family, is not only possible but necessary.

Silko employs other personal relationships in the *Almanac* to comment on power relations on a larger social scale. The relationship between Menardo and Tacho, in particular, bears looking into, because it characterizes Silko's refusal of an identity politics based on a universal Native American identity and her concept of the relationship between gender and resistance strategy.

Menardo is the quintessential self-made man, "which mean[s]," his wife puts it, that he is "a man of darker skin and lower class who had managed to amass a large fortune," in part by denying his Indian blood (*Almanac* 277). Tacho joins Menardo's employ as a chauffeur, and a close, one-sided relationship develops between them, a relationship based on Menardo's fear of and attraction to Tacho's Indianness. Since Menardo considers Tacho essentially a nonperson, and since class boundaries separate their social universes, Menardo divulges his most private fears and desires from the back seat as Tacho drives him to golf dates and luncheons with local political bosses and international arms dealers. As political violence increases all around them, Menardo develops an increasing dependence on Tacho, who, unbeknownst to Menardo, is one of the twin Yaqui brothers who will become the spiritual leaders of the revolution. Tacho has little interest in armed uprising. He believes that the most significant battles of the revolution will be fought and won in the realm of dreams. He has the power to divine the future from dreams and to influence the dreams of others, and he sets to work on Menardo's nightmares. In Menardo's company, Tacho plays the role of the ignorant superstitious Indian. Silko inverts this stereotype by portraying Menardo, the Indian who denies his Indianness and embraces the oppressor's power and technology, as the fatally ignorant superstitious Indian.

As Menardo's reliance on Tacho increases, so does his reliance on a bulletproof vest he is given by an arms dealer. At first he wears the vest only in public. Then he begins to wear it around the estate, and soon he is sleeping in it, and his wife is sleeping in another room. He becomes convinced that it is a talisman that will protect him from all harm, including his own nightmares. Menardo devises a sort of a test of faith—of his faith in the vest—in which he will require Tacho to fire a pistol at his [Menardo's] chest. He is entirely confident that the vest will stop the bullet. At a prearranged time and place, in the presence of a bevy of witnesses, Tacho reluctantly fires, after Menardo commands him to several times, and the bullet pierces the vest and Menardo's heart. To the witnesses, it appears that Menardo, who has allied himself with the oppressors of his people and has put all his faith in their technology, essentially kills himself, while Tacho merely allows him to do it. Both ancient prophecy (the colonizers will do themselves in, Indians need only be patient and wait for it to happen) and contemporary power relations are played out in Tacho and Menardo's relationship. Menardo does do himself in, but Tacho is not exactly a passive instrument. He has worked a potent conjure on Menardo's dreams, and the terror spills out of the nightmares and into Menardo's waking hours; thus, he relies on the vest for protection. In the narrative of Menardo's rise and fall, Silko demonstrates that "Indian blood" does not determine identity — that class status is a more significant determinant; that the oppressors' defenses (the bulletproof vest) are not impenetrable; and that there are means of resistance other than armed uprising.

Like other dissenting fictions—especially David Bradley's—the *Almanac* works against a model of masculinity in which man controls the natural environment by the use of force. Menardo represents this model, Tacho opposes it. Menardo has a mansion carved out of the jungle and a team of gardeners to keep the jungle at bay. He fears the natural world.

It is important to note that the novel critiques a specific white European model of maleness, which Menardo has adopted, not "men" or even "white men." It is a mindset, not a sexual difference or a gender; it is something that we might call the "White Man" way of being. It is a way of being that embodies the characteristics of the epoch of the Death-Eye Dog. In the construction of this mentality, Silko inverts the colonial construction of Native Americans as "savages"; in the *Almanac* the colonizers are the savages.

The White Man way of being emphasizes the construction and maintenance of borders, boundaries, and dualities. Calabazas sees it as a fixation on "[i]maginary lines. Imaginary minutes and hours. Written law" (216). Root sees the imposition of standards of normalcy as crucial to its perpetuation (201). Yoeme sees its essence as anti-spiritual:

> The white man hated to hear anything about spirits because spirits were already dead and could not be tortured and butchered and shot, the only way the white man knew how to deal with the world. Spirits were immune to the white man's threats and to his bribes of money and food. The white man only knew one way to control himself or others and that was with brute force. (581)

Zeta "marvel[s] at the hatred white men harbored for all women, even their own" (704). The White Man way of being is dependent on the strict maintenance of male/female and masculine/feminine dualities.

In the construction of several male characters of various racial and ethnic backgrounds, Silko presents alternatives to the White Man model. In Roy/Rambo, Clinton, Sterling, Root, and Calabazas, Silko suggests alternative masculinities. All of these men adopt a "feminine" mode of storytelling and perceive themselves as collective rather than individual agents.[3] They see what Bob Dubois in *Continental Drift* did not: they see themselves in relation to social and economic structures. They are aware of their class status and they employ it as a site of resistance. Tacho is the *Almanac*'s most well developed embodiment of an alternative to the White Man way of being, and his relative freedom from the constraints of Western models of masculinity is integral to his construction as a resisting subject.

Tacho does not become a spiritual leader of the revolution by force, nor through competition with other males, nor even by choice. He is chosen by two macaws, emissaries from the spirit world and representatives of the natural world. His relationship to the macaws, and by extension to the natural world, revolves around the concept of balance, not conquest. The macaws choose him, he does not control them.

> When the spirits called, Tacho had to go to them . . . . The macaws had come with a message for humans, but it would take awhile for Tacho to understand. The macaws had been sent because this was a time of great change and danger. (476)

The macaws have a number of symbolic functions. Silko links them symbolically with fire and with electricity, crucial means by which the military wing of the resistance hopes to displace state power. Although macaws are tropical birds and are not native to the Pueblos, Silko is drawing on Pueblo mythology and its association of macaws with the sun and with Southern tribal peoples who traded the birds and their feathers (which were used for ceremonial purposes) with the Pueblo people, who have kept macaws in their villages from at least 1100 A. D. (Tyler, *Pueblo Birds* 17).[4] The association of the birds with Southern (Mexican) tribal people is central to the *Almanac*, both structurally and rhetorically. The birds symbolize the connection between Southern tribal people and those of North America, a connection that is crucial to the *Almanac*'s resistance strategy. By the *Almanac*'s end, thousands of unarmed Native pilgrims have joined Tacho and his twin brother El Feo in a long march North, where the macaws tell them they will reclaim Native lands. An armed native resistance, organized chiefly by women, waits in the hills to intervene if the pilgrims are fired upon.

> The leadership of the people's revolt reflects what Edith Swan calls Laguna rules for the acquisition of [gendered] identity. . . . *Social identity passes through women.* Clans and extended families are matrilineal; in other words, descent is traced through women, so a child belongs to the clan of the mother. . . . However, children belong to the ceremonial chamber, the kiva, and dance group of their father . . . . *Religious identity and access to ideology formally pass through men.* The development of identity, therefore, necessitates an integration between these bilateral threads of gender-specific behavior and knowledge. ("Laguna Symbolic Geography" 235-236, italics Swan's)

Appropriately, then, the twin brothers Tacho and El Feo lead the spiritual pilgrims who march north, fulfilling the prophesy of the return of colonized lands, and two women—La Escapía and Zeta—lead the socialist/tribalist military wing of the people's army.[5] It is important to note that this is in accordance with a Pueblo perspective on gender roles and that Silko does not put the women in charge of arms and organizing in order to make a feminist statement about the necessity of women taking power from men. She emphasizes that in Pueblo culture, women have always enjoyed certain freedoms and rights that Western feminists

are struggling to gain. A Pueblo conception of gender is central to the
Almanac's resistance strategy.

La Escapía and Zeta, like the macaws, represent the kinship between
tribal people living in what is now the U. S. and those in Mexico. Silko
makes this connection again and again, arguing that the tribal people
who went North did so to escape the bloodletting and blood sacrifice of
their Southern kin, who were in league with the European conquistadors, and who had, in fact, called the Europeans to the Americas:

> The appearance of the Europeans had been no accident; the
> Gunadeeyahs [sorcerers] had called for their white brethren to join
> them. Sure enough the Spaniards had arrived in Mexico fresh from
> the Church Inquisition with appetites whetted for disembowelment
> and blood. No wonder Cortés and Moctezuma had hit it off together
> when they met; both had been members of the same secret clan. (759)

> The people who refused to join the Gunadeeyahs had fled; the issue
> had been the sorcerers' appetite for blood, and their sexual arousal
> from killing. (759)

In placing Zeta, now an "Arizona Indian" with roots among Mexico's
Yaqui people, and La Escapía, a Yaqui from the Chiapas region, at the
forefront of the people's resistance movements, North and South,
respectively, Silko emphasizes the possibilities for reunification, for
Pan-American resistance efforts.[6]

A Pueblo conception of the cultural meaning of "woman" is central
to an understanding of the *Almanac*'s resistance strategy. The reader
comes to comprehend the *Almanac*'s complex structure of power relations through the stories of female characters in the resistance movement and within the colonialist power structure. The Yaqui grandmother Yoeme occupies the center of the narrative, although she is not present in most of its pages. Like the absent mothers in Morrison's *Jazz*,
Yoeme represents the absent presence of history. She is the link
between her granddaughters and their people's past, since their mother
fails in that role.

Yoeme is the sort of resistance warrior that legends are made of. She
first appears to her twin mixed-blood granddaughters, Lecha and Zeta,
when they are children. Unaware of her grandmother's identity and of

her own Indian heritage, one of the twins whispers to the other that the old woman is an Indian. Her first words to them are the exclamation, "'*You* are Indians!'" (114). She tells them that she never forgot her connection to them: "'All these years I have waited to see if any of you grandchildren might have turned out human. I would come around every so often, take a look'" (118). Here Silko inverts the colonizer's claim that Indians are less than human. The girls apparently pass the humanity test, and Yoeme proceeds to impart her wisdom to them and to draw them away from their large mixed-blood family. Their mother is presented as weak, both emotionally and physically, and ailing, and the girls readily transfer their allegiances to the mysterious and powerful Yoeme.

The conflict between the twins and their mother is the result of cultural and not personal alienation. It is the expression of a persistent concern Silko shares with many Native American writers, a concern summed up by Patricia Clark Smith in an essay about Native American Women's poetry, with the conflict between "the way" and "the way things are" (125), "the way" being traditional tribal cultural ways, and the way things are being the departure from these brought on by colonial and neocolonial influences. Lecha and Zeta grow apart from their mother and shift their allegiances toward Yoeme because their mother has eschewed her Indian heritage in favor of the colonizer's ways and language, and she has become weak and subservient to men as a result. Smith compares contemporary American Indian women's writing with that of Euro-American women and notes that when Euro-American women write about mother-daughter conflict they write about personal conflict and psychological alienation, while American Indian women writers tend to

> see personal discord between women as a matter of cultural alienation. A female relative—a mother, for example—may seem strange, not because she is a Medusa or a harpy . . . but because the daughter literally cannot speak to her, since the mother's language and ways are literally, not just metaphorically, different from the ways of the daughter. Language, custom, and geographical environment, rather than psychological barriers, effect the separation between the generations. (115)

I would add that this statement seems true, in general, of Native American women's fiction as well as poetry. The *Almanac* is a case in point. Silko's construction of gender is intertwined with her resistance strategy, and it grows out of her experience as a Laguna woman. In failing to teach her daughters "the ways" of her Indian culture, the twins' mother has failed in a her role of cultural instructor. This sort of cultural alienation does not generally arise between Euro-American mothers and daughters. As Smith notes, "Anglo" women writers "often show a marked fear of the older woman who will insist on telling others what to do" (119), while Native American women writers *expect* mothers and grandmothers to instruct them in the traditional ways.[7] In divorcing herself from traditional ways, the twins' mother privileges a culture in which women are considered weak and inferior to men over her Native, comparatively gender-egalitarian culture. Silko makes it clear, in an interview, that

> the need for . . . escape [from male domination] is the need of a woman in middle-America, a white Anglo, the WASP woman. In the Pueblo, the lineage of the child is traced through the mother, so it's a matrilineal system. The houses are the property of the woman, not the man. The land is generally passed down through the female side . . . . The kinds of things that cause white upper-middle class women to flee the home for awhile to escape or get away from domination and powerlessness and inferior status, *vis-avis* the husband, and the male, those kinds of forces are not operating . . .   ("A Leslie Marmon Silko Interview" 97)

As is the case in Silko's earlier writings, almost all of the women in the *Almanac* are constructed on a Laguna model. Even the women who work and sleep with the military officers and wealthy entrepreneurs who represent the oppressive colonial influence are more powerful than their men in the private sphere of the home, and, in many cases, in the public spheres of government and the marketplace. Alegría, an architect and Menardo's second wife, and Leah Blue, Tucson real estate tycoon, are representative examples. Both characters are self-centered, greedy, and unconcerned with the plight of the poor. They wield considerable power and are in no way subservient to their men. Both are connected to the realm of real estate; they do not *keep* house, they *con-*

struct homes and buy and sell land. Silko demonstrates a palpable leniency for these characters. While their male counterparts are killed off or emasculated, the women not only escape similar fates, they prosper.

Seese is an exception to the strong female model. She is a drug-addicted, alcoholic former stripper with little self-regard. She has bounced from one abusive man's home to another, unanchored to place, land, or family. If we recall that place is crucial to identity formation in Silko's schema, and that Silko attributes the crimes the colonizers committed during the Native American genocide to the fact that they had no tribe, no village, no family, and no community to censure their behavior, Seese seems more representative of the malaise of postcolonial white America than any other female character in the book. She has no roots in place or culture.

A curious interdependent relationship develops between Seese and Lecha. Seese stays with Lecha because she has nowhere else to go and because she nurses the hope that Lecha will locate her missing child. Lecha depends on Seese to administer her daily injections of various narcotics that ostensibly dull the pain from the "cancer" she may or not have. More importantly, Lecha entrusts Seese with the task of transcribing the ancient codices on a word processor.

Silko's general fondness for her female characters and her delegation of the transcription task to Seese indicates that her resistance strategy leaves open the possibility of a cross-cultural collaboration between women that does not efface difference. This possibility is reflected in Silko's statement (cited above) that "community is tremendously important. That's where a person's identity has to come from, not from racial blood quantum levels" ("Stories and Their Tellers" 19).

Thus far in my reading of the *Almanac*, I have focused on the manner in which Silko employs stories of interpersonal relationships to comment on historical relations between Native Americans and the colonizers of the Americas, and to lay out a Pueblo, egalitarian conception of gender that is central to her resistance strategy. In the next segment, I focus on the relationship between these stories and the constitution of history, addressing a crucial component of resistance strategy that the *Almanac* shares with David Bradley's work and with Leslie Feinberg's *Stone Butch Blues*: the critical role of discourse in the recovery of history and the construction of identity.

At the core of the *Almanac*'s tribal epistemology, as well as its ontology, is a tribal perspective on the function and significance of narrative discourse. A fragment from Silko's imaginative reconstruction of the Mayan codices defines "[n]arrative as analogue for the actual experience, which no longer exists; a mosaic of memory and imagination" (574). Silko's "mosaic" perspective on narrative is distinctly different from the Western idea that narratives may be constructed from a pastiche of memory and imagination. It involves a nonlinear perspective on time.

Wallace Martin, surveying recent theories of narrative, all of them Western, concludes that, "[in] narrative, truth is time-dependent" (76). What he means is that in the Western patriarchal worldview, narrative time is linear, and readers construct truth by discerning a "beginning state," a time of "action," in which elements of the beginning state are acted upon or changed, and, finally, a "refiguration" stage in which "we look back at what happened, tracing the lines that lead to the outcome, discovering why plans did not succeed, how extraneous forces intervened, or how successful actions led to unanticipated results" (Martin 76). "Truth," from this perspective, is the end product, the reader's reward for carefully piecing together the mosaic of linear time that is imbedded in the narrative.

Inherent in Silko's method of storytelling, which de-emphasizes "truth," is a rejection of the notion that narrative "truth" is time-dependent. Paula Gunn Allen writes that

> [t]he idea that everything has a starting point and an ending point reflects accurately the process by which industry produces goods . . . .
> Chronological organization also supports allied western beliefs that the individual is separate from God, that life is an isolated business, and that the person who controls the events around him is a hero. (149)

Allen argues that these beliefs "[contrast] sharply with a ceremonial time sense that assumes the individual as a moving event shaped by and shaping human and nonhuman surroundings" (149). The tribal ceremonial sense of time Allen addresses mirrors the natural world, in which time is seasonal or cyclical. "The traditional tribal concept of time," she asserts, "is timelessness" (147). Tribal time measures "how the person meshes with the revolving of the seasons, the land, and the mythic reality that shapes all life into significance" (154). Allen discusses the "achronicity" of contemporary Native American fiction, a sense of time "in which the individual and the universe are 'tight,'" and which is "not ignorant of the future any more than it is unconscious of the past" (150). She then proceeds to make a connection that Silko makes somewhat less directly in the *Almanac*, the connection between narrative time, history, and colonization:

> There is a connection between factories and clocks, and there is a connection between colonial imperialism and factories. There is also a connection between telling Indian tales in chronological sequence and the American tendency to fit Indians into the slots they have prepared for us. The Indians used to be the only inhabitants of the Americas, but times change. Having perceived us as belonging to history, they are free to . . . re-create us in their history-based understanding, and dismiss our present lives as archaic and irrelevant to the times. (151)

The Western linear perspective on time is embraced by capitalists and Marxists alike. I bring in these ideologies at this point because the rejection of capitalism and a limited borrowing from Marxism figure prominently in the *Almanac*'s discourse of resistance. From the Marxist perspective, history is a linear march toward a just society, toward progress, albeit a very different sort of progress than that embraced by capitalists. This perspective on history conflicts with the *Almanac*'s tribal sense of time and history. Speaking of the original, existing Mayan codices (as opposed to those she creates in the novel), Silko told an interviewer that

> [t]he Mayan people. . . believed that a day was a kind of being and it had a . . . we would maybe say a personality, but that it would return. It might not return for five thousand or eight thousand years, but they believed that a day exactly as it had appeared before would appear again. It's a view that basically denies a lot of western notions about linear time, death, simultaneous planes of existence, and so on." ("A Leslie Marmon Silko Interview" 104)

This perspective is echoed in the *Almanac* by the character El Feo, Tacho's twin brother and co-leader of the spiritual pilgrims who march North.

The days, months, and years were living beings who roamed the starry universe until they came around again. In the Americas, the white man never referred to the past but only to the future. The white man didn't seem to understand that he had no future because he had no past, no spirits of ancestors here. (313)

From the traditional tribal point of view then, Marxism, like capitalism, embraces what Paula Gunn Allen calls a "history-based" linear sense of time rather than a cyclical ceremonial time sense.

Still, the *Almanac*'s resistance strategy utilizes certain components of Marxism. As Ward Churchill puts it, those involved in Native American resistance struggles cannot afford to reject Marxism carte blanche, if for no other reason than that any resistance struggle necessarily involves alliances with like-minded others, and "Marxism possesse[s] . . . a literal hegemony over American radical consciousness" (7). La Escapía attends a Mexican Cuban-financed Marxist bootcamp, yawning her way through much of it while extracting the elements that mesh with her tribal worldview. She finds the Marxists arrogant, sexist, and mindlessly dogmatic, but she accepts their arms shipments and financial support. La Escapía accuses the Euro-American colonizers of genocide and the Marxists of "crimes against tribal histories" (*Almanac* 525). She clearly sees the limits of Marxism's value to Native American resistance struggles, but she sees the applications as well, and—most importantly—she differentiates Marx's works from Marxism as it has been practiced by governments. She notes that "[c]ommune and communal were words that described the lives of many tribes and their own [Yaqui] people as well, that tribal people were already practicing the communal way of being that Marxist revolutions sought. "What was grown, what was caught or raised or discovered, was divided equally and shared all around" 314). Silko has emphasized the communal nature of Pueblo life in interviews. When her childhood house needed replastering, she told an interviewer, for example, a crew of women from the Pueblo came and did the work. Families helped out other families at harvest time, working on the principle of from each according to his abilities, to each according to his need ("A Leslie Marmon Silko Interview" 95). This communalism is effaced by

Marxists who call Native Americans primitive precapitalists.[8] Not even Marx," asserts La Escapía, "had fully understood the meaning of the spiritual and tribal communes of the Americas" (314).

La Escapía learns that Marx was aware of the "crimes of slaughter and slavery committed by the European colonials" against the indigenous peoples of the Americas in the name of capitalism—although it was not then called that (315). Reading Marx, she finds that he has kept these stories—this history—alive. To La Escapía, "[t]his man Marx had understood that the stories or 'histories' are sacred; that within `history' reside relentless forces, powerful spirits, vengeful, relentlessly seeking justice" (316). She imagines Marx as a storyteller, and repositions his work, moving it out of what Paula Gunn Allen would call an "industrial" time frame and into what Allen calls a tribal or "ceremonial" time frame. Reading Marx's histories as stories, La Escapía interprets his work as arguing that "history would catch up with you; it was inevitable, it was relentless. The turning, the changing, were inevitable" (316). She recalls that

> the old people had stories that said much the same, that it was only a matter of time and things European would fade from the American continents. History would catch up with the white man whether the Indians did anything or not . . . . Angelita La Escapía imagined Marx as a storyteller who worked feverishly to gather together a magical assembly of stories to cure the suffering and evils of the world by the retelling of the stories. Stories of depravity and cruelty were the driving force of the revolution, not the other way around. (316)

From La Escapía's—and Silko's—perspective, discourse is the engine that drives the revolution; the revolution does not "produce" discourse, as in Foucault's model. La Escapía takes what she finds useful from Marx and positions it within a tribal time frame, in which history is indistinguishable from any other type of story, and history repeats itself:

> Marx, tribal man and storyteller; Marx with his primitive devotion to the workers' stories. No wonder the Europeans hated him! Marx had gathered official government reports of the suffering of English factory workers the way a tribal shaman might have, feverishly working to bring together a powerful, even magical, assembly of stories. In the repetition of the workers' stories lay a great power . . . . Marx, more

tribal Jew than European, instinctively knew the stories, or "history,"
accumulated momentum and power. (520)

The almanac itself—and here I am using "almanac" to represent
both Silko's novel as a whole and the fragments of the Mayan codices
that she constructs within the novel—functions in the same way as the
"stories" by Marx that La Escapía addresses. Silko uses poetic repetition, repeating the stories of slavery and colonization from the mouths
of a variety of speakers, and in the fragments of the codices as well,
always emphasizing resistance, not domination. The poststructuralist
problematization of history, the problem of locating historical truth, is
decentered, from this tribal perspective, because history does not carry
the burden of truth-telling any more than any other form of narrative.
It is in the stories of history, in their repetition, inversion, and revision,
that power resides; the truthfulness of the narrative is not at issue.
This perspective on history may be seen as the tribal answer to
Derrida's celebrated pronouncement that there is "nothing beyond the
text," which has been taken by some readers to mean that "history"
exists only on the page and has no connection to past reality, which
becomes, in this model, irretrievable (158). From the tribal perspective that Allen and Silko delineate, history exists in the story, and the
story is the discourse that drives revolutions. There is "nothing
beyond the text," because the text, as it travels from mouth to mouth
or in written form, encompasses all that it touches.

The Almanac of the Dead consists of many kinds of stories, and, as
Silko has noted, it "go[es] a bit into the future," into the realm of
prophecy ("A Leslie Marmon Silko Interview" 105). Prophecy, from
Silko's perspective, is simply another kind of story. It is not a story
that *predicts*, as in the Western model, it is a story that *causes* events
to take place. A memorable example of this causal relationship can be
found in Silko's *Ceremony*. Old Betonie tells Tayo that white people
are not all-powerful; although their capability for destruction is
immense, they can be "deal[t] with" by Indians because Indians
"invented white people" (132). He then proceeds to recite for Tayo
the story of the Indian story that created white people. It was at a
gathering of sorcerers, a sort of a competition to see who could out-
evil whom, long before the colonization of the Americas. After all of
the other sorcerers had demonstrated their tricks and wares, the last

one stood in the shadows and began to chant the story of "white skin
people/like the belly of a fish/covered with hair" emerging from their
caves across the water and coming to the Americas in swarms (135).
The story goes on to chronicle the ensuing destruction of tribal people
and the environment. The other sorcerers award the storyteller first
prize but tell "it" (its gender isn't known) that its story "isn't so
funny/It doesn't sound so good," and that the story should be taken
back. The sorcerer in the shadows replies that the story is "already
turned loose/ It's already coming./It can't be called back" (138).
There is "nothing beyond the text," no point outside of the story from
which it can be "called back." As I note in section one, above, and
address in more detail below, the story of the Indian witches who
"call" the Destroyers/colonizers to the Americas is repeated in the
Almanac. The narrative empowers Native Americans by holding them
responsible for the "invention" of the colonizers. What was done, it is
implied, will be undone. What—or who, in this case—was conjured
up by the act of storytelling will be undone by a story. A fragment
from the fictional codice foretells this undoing.

> One day a story will arrive in your town. There will always be dis-
> agreement over direction—whether the story came from the southwest
> or the southeast. The story may arrive with a stranger, a traveler
> thrown out of his home country months ago. Or the story may be
> brought by an old friend, perhaps the parrot trader. But after you hear
> the story, you and the others prepare by the new moon to rise up
> against the slave masters. (*Almanac* 578)

As in the story from *Ceremony* that set the colonization process in
motion, the identity of the teller of the tale is unimportant. Stories—and
history—the *Almanac* argues, don't belong to their tellers; they are set
in motion, told and retold, and re-enacted. This perspective on the function of narrative is possible only within a "ceremonial" time-frame. It
is a perspective that foregrounds interpersonal agency and de-emphasizes the role of the individual agent. Silko's characters who have managed to stay grounded in their tribal identities, then, have an understanding of interactive agency that Banks's Bob Dubois never acquires
and that Morrison's characters embrace after struggle.

Like the story of the Gunadeeyahs calling the colonizers to the Americas, the narrative of the four Geronimos reflects the *Almanac*'s ceremonial time perspective and relates it directly to the production of history. The Yaqui Calabazas recalls the Geronimo story as it was told to him by tribal elders. In keeping with the open-ended, communal tribal way of story-making, Calabazas is given the task of adding to the story as it is being told to him. To make a long story short, the elders are discussing the historical figure Geronimo, as he was constructed by the colonial military and the media of his time. They note that these institutions produced Geronimo through narrative and photographs. The problem with the white man's history of Geronimo, from the Yaqui perspective, is that Geronimo was not one but four to seven different Apache men who at one time or another were identified as Geronimo, a name that never belonged to any of them to begin with. When Mexican soldiers went into battle, they called out "Geronimo," to enlist the aid of St. Jerome. But "the U. S. soldiers . . . misunderstood [this] just as they had misunderstood just about everything else they had found in this land," and misapplied the name to an Apache raider who they mythologized as embodying the resistance effort, although there was no one such warrior (224).

Over time, several "Geronimos" were captured or otherwise coerced into being photographed. The photographs all look like the same warrior but, inexplicably, they do not resemble any of the actual Apaches who are photographed. Viewing the photographs, the white men interpret the "little smudges and marks like animal tracks across the snow" on the paper (227). The Yaqui elders describe photographic images in much the same way that Derrida describes text on a page. The Yaquis see only smudges and tracks; only with "training" do they see the images the white men describe. But they note that even among the white men, there is disagreement over how well the image "represents" the person being photographed. This indeterminacy causes the white men great anxiety, but the Yaquis see it simply as alternative readings of the same text or story, the sum of which *are* the story. The text of the photograph, from their perspective, serves multiple functions and is subject to multiple—but not necessarily competing and cancelling—interpretations. The elders explain the whites' insistence on a linear history of Geronimo that meshes with their worldview and their colonial designs this way: "[W]hites put great store in names. But once the whites had a name for a thing, they seemed unable ever again to recognize the thing itself" (224).

The prophetic quality of storytelling in the *Almanac* extends beyond the borders of the text, a fact that must not be lost on Silko now that the "real" has come into alignment with her fictional construction of it. The novel portrays/predicts at least two significant events which have recently come to pass: the Zapatista National Liberation Army's uprising against the Mexican government in Chiapas—in which, incidentally, one "Comandante Tacho" figures prominently—and the rising up of the homeless against the center of Capitalist patriarchal power.[9] The former event occurred in 1992-93 and again in 1994-95, several years after the publication of the *Almanac* (1991). In 1994, a homeless man was shot to death on the White House lawn by police who claimed he intended to kill the president. After the incident, journalists uncovered a pattern of police harassment of the area homeless—many of them Vietnam-era veterans—that had inspired an organized resistance.

In the final segment of this chapter, I turn to the body. The diverse components of Silko's resistance strategy are all grounded in the centrality of the body—of the embodied subject—to history; hence, I look to Silko's representation of the body to bring together the key elements of my reading.

The human body—its surfaces and its interiors, its component parts, its fluids, its sex and its sexuality, its sensitivity to pain, its life and its death—is a continuously explored presence in the *Almanac*. Silko inserts into history a subject that is profoundly and unquestionably—if not unproblematically—embodied. Leslie Adelson asks,

> [W]hat is history if not the account of human bodies over time? History without bodies is unimaginable. How odd then that the grand abstraction of history would seem to obliterate the very concrete stuff of which it is made . . . . The alleged dichotomy between historical abstractions and the concrete bodies whose stories they tell rests on the exclusion of human subjects from both poles: history becomes its own subject in the abstraction, and bodies are mere objects on what Hegel calls the "slaughterbench" of history. (1)

Adelson goes on to assert that "[h]istory does not happen *to* people; it is a function of the relationships among human bodies, which are themselves historically constituted" (22, italics Adelson's).

Contemporary theorists sometimes seem more interested in the processes through which the body and history are reconstituted in narrative discourse than in bodies themselves—as actors, as agents, and as subjects. In the section above, I have addressed Silko's rejection of the discourse/history binary, and her perspective on the nature of narrative discourse. In this section, I address her emphasis on the human body— as the object of oppression, as an historical agent, and as a resisting subject—an emphasis that some readers have found unsettling. First, I will treat Silko's concern with the body as the object and the site of colonial oppression, and her focus on the relationship between the Western notion of mind/body duality and colonial aggression. I will then examine her problematization of sexuality, and, finally, I will address her focus on resisting bodies.

The subjectivity that Silko constructs in the *Almanac* is precisely the sort of "embodied subjectivity" or "psychical corporeality" that Elizabeth Grosz suggests, in *Volatile Bodies*, feminist thinkers need to begin imagining. The *Almanac*'s subject matter—resistance to colonial oppression—necessitates its engagement with the Western patriarchal mindset, of which mind/body duality and the privileging of the mind/masculine dimension are prominent features.[10] Silko makes clear the manner in which colonizers have exploited mind/body binaries in the service of their aggression. Essentially, the colonial mentality constructs patriarchal colonizers as representatives of the mind, the masculine, and reason. The colonized—and the resistance—are constructed in this model as bodies, as feminine, and as irrational.

The colonizers' construction of the indigenous inhabitants of the Americas as somehow more embodied, and hence more "brute" served some very practical purposes: it rationalized and perpetuated the enslavement of Native Americans, which took place on a grand scale, and it invalidated their complex systems of knowledge and "necessitated" the importation of Christianity. Silko emphasizes the role of Western notions of the body in the perpetuation of these practices and the fact that Western narratives of the "discovery" of the Americas efface the fact that colonization involves brutal aggression against very real bodies, who in turn function as *embodied* resisting subjects.

One technique Silko uses to insert bodies into history is the cataloguing of acts of Native American resistance and colonial acts of aggression against the bodies of Native Americans. In La Escapía's speech at the public trial of the Marxist Bartolomeo, for "Crimes Against Tribal Histories," she chants names, dates, places, and most importantly, for our purposes here, numbers of bodies dead or freed. In the introduction to this chapter, I cite La Escapía's "figures for the Native American holocaust" from this speech.

> 1500—72 million people lived in North, Central, and South America.
> 1600—10 million people live in North, Central, and South America. '
> (530)

These figures fall at the end of a list three pages long. The effect of this cataloguing is the re-embodiment of historical subjects. As Leslie Adelson notes in her discussion of German National Socialism and genocide, "The abbreviation 'six million' is as effective as it is . . . not merely because the figure is astronomical or frequently repeated, but because it signifies in no uncertain terms the ineluctable embodiment of history" (23). This is precisely the effect of Silko's frequent insertion into the text of numbers of bodies lost to colonial aggression.

The *Almanac* embodies the history of colonialism at every turn, never allowing the reader to forget the human price that colonialism extracts or the human bodies that resist it. Silko traces the effects of the colonial mentality and its mind/body masculine/feminine dualities from the earliest contact between Indians and Europeans to the present. At this point, I will introduce Elizabeth Grosz's observations on the alienation that accompanies these dualities. I see striking parallels between Grosz's observations and the *Almanac*'s construction of the masculine colonial and neocolonial mentalities. Grosz suggests that in Western cultures permeated by notions of mind/body duality, men "attempt to distance themselves from the very kind of corporeality—uncontrollable, excessive, expansive, disruptive, irrational—that they have attributed to women" (200). She cites as examples of this phenomenon

> men's capacity to distance themselves, their subjectivities, from their sexualities in such a way that men (both gay and straight) regard their sexual desires as overwhelming or uncontrollable impulses. . . . men's capacity to reify bodily organs, to be interested in organs rather than the subjects to whom they belong, to seek sexuality without intimacy, to strive for anonymity amid promiscuity, to detach themselves from sex-

ual engagement in order to establish voyeuristic distance, to enjoy witnessing and enacting violence and associate it with sexual pleasure. . .
(200)

If we substitute "colonizers (and their descendants) for "men" in this passage and "Native peoples" for "women," we have a very accurate description of the alienation that Silko depicts as affecting (or *in*fecting) every facet of the lives of colonizers and their descendants, as described in the *Almanac*—an alienation that is produced by mind/body oppositions.[11] The present-day descendants of colonizers in the *Almanac* traffic in illicit human organs and pornographic materials that depict torture and surgical mutilation of bodies, they achieve sexual gratification not through actual contact with other consenting human bodies but as a result of viewing live government torture videos (Beaufrey), of listening over telephone lines to the sounds of murder-for-hire on the other end (Max Blue) or of engaging in sex with animals (Judge Arne) or children (General J).

The impulse to dissociate from the body, to fragment it, and to associate sexual pleasure with violence is perhaps most compellingly embodied in Trigg, the parapalegic illicit blood- and organ-bank magnate. Trigg's physical state is a heavy-handed metaphor for the oppressor's separation of "self" and body. He envisions himself as superior to members of the working class, people of color, and women, all of whom he sees as more embodied than he is. Trigg experiences no sensation from the waist down. He achieves erections with the aid of a machine. The only human being he experiences sexual pleasure with is the wife of a murderer; the pleasure is derived from the knowledge that he may become the murderer's victim. He vampirically increases the stores of blood in the bank's freezers by draining blood from immobilized homeless men, whom he sexually violates as he murders.

Not surprisingly, critics have been a bit unsettled by Silko's depiction of white Euro-American males. She is not, however, is not simply depicting white Euro-American maledom as a bestial blood-hungry boys' club, she is constructing Euro-American males exactly as their ancestors constructed the "savages" they encountered in the Americas. She is also constructing the descendants of colonizers in the mold of their ancestors, who, inarguably, were traffickers in human flesh, and were subject, as she puts it to, "all the terrible compulsions and hungers aroused by owning human slaves," and none of the community censure they left behind in Europe with their families (425).[12]

In the *Almanac*, alienation and fragmentation are central themes; white men in particular, and Indian men who have adopted their ways, like Menardo, suffer from a common malady. Chief among its symptoms is the sense of separation from and compartmentalization of one's body and one's sexuality. These feelings cause the specific "symptoms" in the Almanac's cast of alienated wealthy men that I cite Elizabeth Grosz's treatment of above: the reification of bodily organs, sexuality without intimacy, anonymity amid promiscuity, and voyeuristic pleasure associated with sexual violence. The descendants of sorcerers, it seems, have ensorcelled themselves.

In the Reign of the Death-Eye Dog, alienation from and fragmentation of the body are the order of the day. Hence, sexual relations are problematized in the *Almanac*. With few exceptions, sexual relations are presented in one (or both) of two ways: as commercial exchanges or as aggressive acts involving violence or coercion. The two scenes below are representative of heterosexual sex in the *Almanac*. In both cases, women exchange sex with men for services rendered (Seese and the lawyer) or economic power conferred (Zeta and Mr. Coco, who has just given her a promotion).

The lawyer pumps above her as if he is doing push-ups, a brief down-curve and thrust before he rises back up, and all Seese can imagine is being fucked by a strange machine. (111)

[A]fter she had undressed, Mr. Coco remained in the armchair merely staring at her breasts. Between his legs in its nest of white pubic hair, the penis lay like a pale grub or caterpillar. It did not move. Although this was to be her first encounter with a man other than Uncle Federico and his fat, dirty fingers, Zeta felt nothing. No fear, no embarrassment, no horror at standing naked in the dingy sales office of Mexico Tours, at five-thirty on a Friday afternoon. The swamp cooler droned in the window behind her and emitted periodic drips into a flat pan on the floor. . . . It seemed like a lot of exertion bouncing around on his lap, having to brace herself against the chair arms with both her knees and her elbows. Mr. Coco moaned and groaned and nibbled away at

her breasts. Zeta thought she should feel some revulsion, but she did
not. She felt sweaty and her legs were cramped, but nothing about the
scene was remarkable. (126)

In both of these scenes, the body is represented in the mechanistic terms
associated with it in Enlightenment thinking. Rather than a superior scientific machine, however, it is a low-budget imperfect machine, an
alienation machine. In the second scene there are obvious parallels
between the dripping swamp cooler and Mr. Coco, and Zeta and the
"flat pan." The women see both their own bodies and those of their
partners as if from a distance, and they see fragmented, not whole, bodies. Affected by the malaise of the Reign of the Death-Eye Dog, both
women see the very act that produces life as mechanistic and devoid of
life. This perspective is characteristic of all of the narratives of sexual
transactions in the *Almanac*.

If heterosexual relations in the *Almanac* are bad, homosexual relations are worse. Heterosexual relations are devoid of vitality and
humor, but homosexual relations are permeated with a lust for death.
Female homosexuality is entirely effaced in the *Almanac*. Its absence
is made especially remarkable by the novel's preoccupation with the
negative depiction of male homosexuality. Gay male relationships are
equated with what Silko apparently views as one of the most repugnant
aspects of late capitalism: the commodification of the body. The gay
threesome Beaufrey, Serlo, and David seem to embody every heinous
detail of the neocolonial mentality. They dabble in eugenics; traffic in
pornography (specializing in videos of Native "sexual initiation" and
the "live" torture of victims of State interrogations); and achieve sexual climax only with the aid of snuff films. Each of the three is capable
of loving only himself and sees himself reflected in the eyes of the
object of his sexual desire. Their coming together as a threesome seems
to multiply their greed and bloodlust, especially in the cases of Beaufrey
and Serlo. The baby that Beaufrey kidnaps, their symbolic son, is murdered by Beaufrey's lackeys, at his command, is videotaped being
butchered, and is sold in fragments for organ transplants. Clearly these
men, more than any other characters, represent the descendants of the
Gunadeeyahs whose reign over the Americas is prophesied in the
codices as the epoch of the Death-Eye Dog.

The other prominent homosexual relationship in the *Almanac* is that of Ferro (Lecha's son) and his white partners Paulie and Jamie. Although they do not engage in the wholesale celebration of the destruction of human life that Beaufrey, Serlo, and David engage in, Ferro, Paulie, and Jamie are locked in a destructive power relationship in which sex and drugs function as currency. Ferro delights in exploiting Paulie's pathetic need, and Paulie is incapable of relating to any human being on an emotional level. Ferro's obsession with Jamie is the result of Ferro's self-hatred. He doesn't want Jamie, he wants to *be* Jamie: white, young, hard-bodied, and blond. He both desires and hates Jamie's "perfect" white, blonde-haired, blue-eyed body (180). When Ferro looks at Paulie, he "remembers playing with chunks of white clay," as a child, "rubbing it over his hands and arms to make himself lighter" (182). Unlike Beaufrey, Serlo, and David, Ferro doesn't see himself reflected in the eyes of his Euro-American lovers, he sees what he is not. Silko deploys homosexuality, in Ferro's case, as a mechanism for racial self-hatred.

Silko's treatment of male homosexuality and the gay male body invites close examination. We must ask why, as a novel concerned with resistance to oppression, the *Almanac* seems determined to ignore entirely the sexual oppression of lesbians and equally determined to present gay men in relentlessly negative terms. The question of why a novel concerned with the valorization of traditional American Indian ways of being seems to have jettisoned traditional American Indian acceptance of homosexuality also bears looking into. Paula Gunn Allen observes that

> [r]ecent scholarly work reveals the universal or nearly universal presence of homosexuality and lesbianism among tribal peoples, the special respect and honor often accorded gay men and women, and the alteration in that status as a result of colonization of the continent by Anglo-Europeans . . . . Homophobia, which was rare (perhaps even absent entirely) among tribal peoples in the Americas, has steadily grown among them as they have traded traditional tribal values for Christian industrial ones. (198)

One of the recent scholarly works Allen cites is Walter W. Williams's *The Spirit and the Flesh: Sexual Diversity in American Indian Culture.*

Williams's well-researched book focuses on male homosexuality and North American Indian cultures, and it documents the widespread acceptance of homosexuality in pre-colonial American Indian communities. Williams finds that the longer and more sustained and oppressive the contact with Europeans and their descendants, the greater the likelihood of negative attitudes toward homosexuality among tribal peoples. A simple answer to the question of why the *Almanac* indulges in the exclusively negative depiction of gay men might be that Silko is a Pueblo Indian (with one Euro-American parent), and that the Pueblos have a long history of contact with Europeans (more than four hundred years). Perhaps, one might think, she has been influenced by the dominant culture's negative attitude toward homosexuality.[13] This answer, however, is a bit too simplistic. Although the Pueblos were among the first of Native North American peoples to experience colonial oppression, and although they have certainly suffered at the hands of the colonial Spanish and later the U. S. government, they have never been conquered, and they have retained a nearly singular degree of autonomy and cultural integrity.[14] White culture has never been "dominant" in the Pueblos. This aside, it is obvious that Silko is aware of the importance of preserving and promoting her traditional Native cultural heritage, in matters pertaining to nearly everything *but* homosexuality.

As I have noted above, heterosexual relations are portrayed in the *Almanac* in nearly as negative a light as gay male relations. Both heterosexual and homosexual relations are dominated by the malaise associated with the Western mind/body duality imported to the Americas with colonialism. Silko's employment of the body and sexual practices as metaphors for the body politic and political practices seems to preclude any portrayal of the body as capable of pleasure, as though this would detract from the power of the metaphor. This does not adequately explain the *Almanac*'s construction of male homosexuality as a solipsistic practice fueled by hatred, however. Heterosexual couplings in the *Almanac* are characterized primarily in terms of indifference and an inability or unwillingness of the participants to connect emotionally. Gay male couplings are characterized by hatred and are ritual enactments of destructive desires. The novel attempts to explain away male homosexuality in the tiredest of terms, as though it were an aberration that required an explanation. Gay men have absent fathers and impossible mothers. They hate their mothers and all women (99, 102-103, 691). Gay men in general are imbued with the qualities that Silko associates with the model of white maleness that is in turn associated with the colonial mentality. It is the same model on which the *Alma*nac constructs those associated with the mechanistic forces of destruction that drive witchery. At the core of sorcerer/gay male/White Man mentality is a sense of displacement and separation from the life force within and without and a fixation on death and destruction.[15] The body, in this mindset, is viewed as alien and sexuality is perceived as an uncontrollable drive. Eric, the only gay man who is not constructed on this model, self-destructs early in the novel. He commits suicide, and the gay men around him rush to exploit his death. David takes lurid color photographs of the corpse, emphasizing the separation of the subject (Eric) from the body. The photos are displayed in a trendy gallery and launch his career as a photographer, which Beaufrey finances.

Silko deploys male homosexuality, it seems, to exaggerate and embody the qualities associated with the colonial mentality and with witchery. The gay male triads in the *Almanac* serve to amplify all of the negative qualities associated with colonial aggression and neocolonial oppression, the characteristics of the epoch of the Death-Eye Dog itself. This is especially unfortunate and ironic given the fact that it was the colonizers who introduced into Native American cultures the notion that homosexuality is perverse and "sinful." Silko's treatment of male homosexuality undercuts her resistance politics.

Despite its treatment of male homosexuality, the *Almanac* is Silko's most accomplished work, to date, of narrative fiction. It is composed of dozens of stories with dozens of tellers and of stories within stories within stories. One story told by Yoeme rather early in the novel embodies and foreshadows—in elegantly concise form—both Silko's emphasis on the living breathing quality of history-as-story, and her focus on the resisting bodies that interact with forces of oppression to create history. Yoeme tells Lecha and Zeta a story that traces a fragment of the textual history of the Mayan codices. No dates are attached to the story, but we know that it takes place after the colonization process is well underway. I will summarize the elements of the story that I want to examine in detail (I want to retain the story's narrative form rather than present it in explicated fragments).

A tribe far to the South, probably in what is now Mexico, realizes that it is about to become extinct, as a result of colonial destruction and slavery. The last survivors debate the fate of the codices now in their possession, "the almanac [that] told them who they were and where they had come from" (246). Some believe that they should allow the almanac to die with them, since it is their history and their story is about to end. Others know that "if even part of their almanac survived, they as a people would return someday" (246). The latter group prevails and four children are chosen to flee to the North with the almanac. One of the youngest children sustains herself by surreptitiously sucking on the edges of the horsegut parchment of the almanac while the others sleep.

Many weeks pass, and the children come upon an abandoned village far to the North populated only by a hunchbacked woman the fleeing inhabitants have left behind. The woman is stirring a thin stew of roots, bulbs, and grubs she has managed to forage. Weak with hunger, the eldest girl covertly tears a page from the almanac and tosses it into the stew. It nourishes the little band, providing strength for the last leg of their journey north. The hunchbacked woman wants more pages for more stews and does not want the children to leave, but they move on, except for the stubborn young girl who had suckled the edges of the pages. The eldest girl goes back to recover the portion of the manuscript that the young girl carried and discovers that the hunchbacked woman has murdered the child. The eldest girl snatches the manuscript pages from the corpse and hurries on. Yoeme concludes the story with the admonition that

> "it had been the almanac that had saved them. The first night, if the
> eldest had not sacrificed a page from the book, that crippled woman
> would have murdered them all right then, while the children were
> weak from hunger and the longer journey." (253)

Silko's rendition of this story illustrates her perspective on the multiple functions of stories in Pueblo culture.[16] The story is not fixed in time; hence, the importance of storytelling as an open-ended process is emphasized. It is a story within a story, emphasizing "the idea that one story is only the beginning of many stories, and the sense that stories never truly end—[this] represents an important contribution of Native

American cultures to the English language" (Silko, "Language and Literature" 84). The story stresses the importance of community: the girl who suckles the edges of the pages surreptitiously endangers the well-being of the tribe; the girl who contributes a page to the stew (after memorizing its contents) for all to share performs an act of sacrifice that ensures the physical continuance of the tribe. The story functions didactically, as do European fairy tales and stories. It teaches children about responsibility and community. The girl who thinks only of her own hunger and remains in the shade of the cottonwood trees with the hunchbacked woman is murdered, the girl who leads the others north becomes a legendary hero. Negative consequences, Silko points out in an essay on Pueblo storytelling, do not function merely to discourage certain behaviors; more importantly, they allow people to accept their own and their family members' mistakes and misfortunes. Stories of terrible misfortune, like the murder of a child, allow people to believe that "if others have endured, so can we" (Silko, "Language and Literature" 86). Additionally, Yoeme's story stresses the connection between the Pueblos (presumably the people in the far North toward whom the children are heading) and the tribes in the South, and it teaches a lesson in geography, the sort of lesson that Silko stresses is still passed on primarily through stories ("Language and Literature" 89). It also includes some important information about the sort of goods that were traded between the Pueblos and their Southern kin. Finally, the story refuses to render its meaning in terms of pat good/evil dualities and simplifications. Yoeme's last words to Lecha and Zeta on the story's meaning are

> The woman had been left behind by the others. The reign of the Death-Eye dog is marked by people like her. She did not start out that way. In the days that belong to Death-Eye Dog, the possibility of becoming like her trails each one of us. (253)

If we examine the story in terms of figurative representations, we find a tale about the meaning, significance, and transmittal of history. The children are each entrusted with a fragment of the codices, with the hope that at least some of the manuscript will reach its destination, and that the children will help each other on their way. History is carried forth by various sources; in their merging and blending the story is revised and continued. The girl who suckles on the edges of the pages in private receives only the most meager form of nourishment. When the page is thrown into the communal stew pot, everyone is well-nourished. History is best understood in the broader contexts of social relations and power relations. History has to be digested by each individual and made into story, meshed with individual and cultural narratives, but it only "nourishes," and yields its richest meaning, in the context of community. Silko would see the poststructuralist claim that history exists only in language, only in the text—that historical truth is inaccessible—as a very narrow, very European way of looking at the story of history. For her, historical narrative is not a category of narrative that exists only on the written page, it is story that has made its way into all sorts of other cultural and personal "stews" (narratives) and is accessible as a living breathing component of culture itself.

Finally, I wish to emphasize the role of the body in Yoeme's story. To do so, we need to exit the realm of the figurative and reenter the story at the literal level. If we were reading figuratively, we might say that the bodies that eat the text of history that provides the tribe's identity are representative of the body politic, of youth and age, of gendered concepts, and so on. It is significant, however, that the story emphasizes the interaction of specific physical bodies with history through the mechanism of the distinctively physical process of digestion. The body is also emphasized in the fact that the manuscript itself is inscribed on a body fragment (horse stomach), in the fact that the children carry the manuscripts beneath their clothing, close to their bodies, and in the fact that Yoeme is telling the tale orally to Lecha and Zeta. Historical narrative does not exist in this story except in its relationship with embodied subjects. It is inscribed onto the stomach of a horse, carried forth by the bodies of the children, and literally taken into the bodies of all of the primary agents in the story. Yoeme makes it clear that if the text were not taken into the bodies of the children and the woman, history would have ceased to exist, because the starving woman would have murdered the children and eaten them and the manuscript. Just as the manuscript predicts that days past will return, will be re-inhabited by embodied subjects at a future time, the manuscript itself is recycled through human bodies. History is created, acted upon, revised, and perpetuated by specific, embodied subjects. It is important to note, too, that all of these actions undertaken by very real bodies become part and substance of history. Yoeme points out that "the story of [the children's] journey had somehow been included in these notebooks" (247). As Leslie Adelson puts it,

> The postmodernist preoccupation with the difficulty, impossibility, undesirability of saying "I" (claiming the imperial rights of the subject) is released from the falsely dichotomized alternative between subject and object as soon as the body comes into sharper focus. For the body is so many things all at the same time. Sometimes the victim of history, it is always the object of historical construction, the site of historical experience, the arbiter of all cognition, and the material ground of freedom. It is a thing and a sign, an inside and an outside, a boundary constantly crossing itself. (34)

Adelson argues—and, on the basis of the evidence presented in this chapter, I concur—that inserting resisting bodies into history allows for more possibilities of resistance:

> If the body, from which neither we nor our cultural projections of the subject can escape, is both within and outside the reach of dominant orders, then resistance to oppression is a matter not of missing heroes beyond the invisible walls of culture but of everyday mortals: you and me, your neighbors on the planet and mine. (34-35).

Like the girl who drops the page into the stew, Silko multiplies the possibilities for resistance by writing bodies into history and history into bodies.

Yoeme's story is a microcosm of the *Almanac of the Dead* as a whole. The *Almanac* is at no point fixed in time. There are references to historical events, and the story has the feel of the present or near future, but its time frame is never fixed. To readers accustomed to traditional Western narrative form, this is initially distressing. We are forced to confront our discomfort and our habitual dependence on "industrial" markers of time. The *Almanac* weaves together many stories, stories within stories and has no ending. The novel's action—the class war for the reclamation of Native lands—does not march forward to a conclusion, nor even to an ambiguous point of closure with several possible interpretations. The novel closes with the pilgrims from the

South still marching and the revolutionary action de-emphasized. We are left with Sterling returning to Laguna Pueblo and quietly mentally piecing together seemingly disparate elements from Pueblo mythology, his geographical surroundings, history, family stories, and his experiences with the twin sisters. The reader is left to do the same.

In the next chapter I address a novel that is much narrower in its focus but that shares Silko's, Bradley's, and Morrison's emphasis on history: Leslie Feinberg's *Stone Butch Blues*. Feinberg explores the means by which gender shapes and constrains agency, and she questions the usefulness of the very notion of gender.

Notes

1.   Silko discusses the functions of stories and storytelling in "Language and Literature from a Pueblo Indian Perspective." I address these functions in the *Almanac* in detail at the close of this chapter.

2.   I address Silko's negative depiction of male homosexuality in the final segment of this chapter.

3.   I refer to the feminine narrative mode, have defined in the previous chapter..

4.   Macaws and parrots have numerous important symbolic associations in Pueblo mythology. Among these are the South, the sun, Corn Mother, salt, and fertility. I have chosen to elaborate on the associations that Silko makes in the *Almanac*. For a more complete cataloguing of the birds' symbolic functions and associations, see Tyler, *Pueblo Birds*.

5.   Twins have special significance in Pueblo myth and legend. See Boas (49, 249, 285). The "Twin Heroes" were with the people from the time of emergence. They perform heroic deeds and function as leaders of the people in times of crisis in a number of Pueblo narratives.

6.   The "Mexican" and "Arizona" distinctions are Sterling's—the Almanac's representative Laguna Pueblo Indian.

7.   Smith, a scholar at the University of New Mexico, uses the term "Anglo" as it is used by New Mexicans, particularly Chicanos and Pueblo people, primarily to denote white people of European descent.

8.   See Russell Means's "The Same Old Song" for a response to Marxists who call Native Americans primitive precapitalists.

9.   The masked Comandante Tacho was featured in an AP photo accompanying an 11 April 1995 AP article titled "Mexico, Guerilla Leaders Agree to Hold Formal Talks," by Anita Snow in the Penn State *Daily Collegian*.

10.   I refer to the traditional Western association of the masculine and the positive with the mind, and the feminine and the negative with the body. Elizabeth Grosz sums it up as follows. "The male/female opposition has been closely allied with the mind/body opposition . . . . [The] mind is rendered equivalent to the masculine and body equivalent to the feminine (thus ruling out women a priori as possible subjects of knowledge . . .)" (14).

11.   I use the term "descendants" here to represent those who have perpetuated, co-opted, or accepted the colonial mentality. The set of the descendants of the colonizers, then, does not necessarily include all of their biological descendants; it is not synonymous with "Europeans" or "European Americans," although all European Americans have benefitted from the privilege bestowed by this dominant mentality.

12.   Silko anticipates the argument that Native Americans in what is now Mexico kept slaves and engaged in human sacrifice when she distinguishes, at numerous points throughout the *Almanac*, between Pueblo people and southern tribal people. She asserts, as I mention earlier, that Aztec practicioners of human sacrifice were psychic allies of the European conquistadors, that they summoned the Europeans to the Americas, and that people of the Pueblos severed relations with the Aztecs over the issue of human sacrifice.

13.   Williams's discusses an incident in 1978 in which a Laguna Pueblo family was effectively broken apart by its homophobia (209).

14.   Joe S. Sando's *Pueblo Nations: Eight Centuries of Pueblo Indian History* provides a concise and highly readable narrative of the Pueblos' successful struggle to retain autonomy. The Pueblos have been influenced, however, by Euro-Christian attitudes about homosexuality. This influence was inevitable, given the Pueblos long and close coexistence with Europeans and European-Americans.

15.   As above, I capitalize White Man here to denote not all white men but the   specific colonial/neocolonial mentality that Silko delineates. As I note early in this chapter, it is not blood or biology but beliefs, values, and sense of community that determine identity for Silko.

16.   See Silko, "Language and Literature from a Pueblo Indian Perspective."

CHAPTER 6

Queering Class:

Leslie Feinberg's Stone Butch Blues

> At the violet hour when the eyes and back
> Turn upward from the desk, when the human engine waits
> Like a taxi throbbing waiting
> I Tiresias, though blind, throbbing between two lives
> Old man with wrinkled female breasts, can see
>
> —T. S. Eliot *The Waste Land*

Leslie Feinberg's first novel, *Stone Butch Blues* (1993) is set largely within what Marjorie Garber calls the "third space" outside of gender binaries (11).[1] In presenting the daily struggles of a working-class transgendered person, a person who fits into neither prescribed gender category, Feinberg's novel exposes the quotidian practices through which fixed gendered and sexual identities are culturally constructed and brutally imposed. *Stone Butch Blues* is a landmark historical novel chronicling pre-Stonewall working-class transgendered and gay and lesbian life and struggles in the urban Northeast and the conflicts between those struggles and the women's liberation movement.

This chapter examines the interrelationship of gendered identity development, socioeconomic structures, and resistance to oppression in *Stone Butch Blues.* I argue that Feinberg foregrounds socioeconomic concerns and class structures, and I examine the novel's mapping of the complex effects of class constraints on gender expression. Since Feinberg's novel is relatively new and issued by a small press, much of the critical discourse addressing it to date has taken place at conferences and on the internet. In these venues, I have found that her focus on class is generally dismissed as old-fashioned, simplistic, and naïve. These claims are not entirely without merit; Feinberg is more Marxist than neoMarxist. However, a critical discipline that has been as slow to address class as has gender theory[2] cannot afford to dismiss the class concerns of an author as uniquely positioned to explore them as Feinberg, who is a transgender activist, a longtime labor organizer and chronicler of labor struggles, a novelist, and an independent scholar of transgender history.

The achievement of Feinberg's award-winning novel is not that it is the first novel to tell the story of a transgendered person, but that it is the first to embrace "transgendered" as an identity.[3] *Stone Butch Blues* addresses a transgendered experience that is just beginning to see the light of day in both the medical and the popular literature on the subject: that of the female-to-male (FTM) transgendered subject.[4] *Stone Butch Blues* makes it clear that FTM expression is a complex identity in its own right. The very terms FTM and MTF are inadequate—Feinberg would argue—in their suggestion that anyone whose gender expression falls outside of either "F" or "M" is moving towards the expression of the "opposite" gender.

Feinberg's novel is the first work of fiction about a transgendered person to interrogate, albeit implicitly, the American Psychiatric Association's official diagnosis of gender identity disorder, or, in common parlance, gender dysphoria: the notion that if one is uncomfortable with one's assigned gender identity, there is something wrong with the one experiencing the discomfort rather than with the cultural institutions doing the assigning.[5] In interrogating the gender dysphoria diagnosis, *Stone Butch Blues* embraces the body and explores its cultural meaning. Feinberg asserts that the "disease" of gender dysphoria infects the dominant culture, and that it is a dis-ease with difference.[6]

The concept of transgender has been seized upon by gender theorists because it possesses the potential to question the entire notion not just of gender identity but of the biological "sex" categories to which gender identity has been wedded. Transgendered subjects exist not in a space outside of gender, but in a space in which gender does not follow naturally from "sex," in which biological sex is a mutable construct.[7] It is important to note, however, that definitions are contested in this realm. Neither transgendered communities nor those who theorize gender speak with a monolithic voice. Not all transgendered subjects, activists, and scholars endorse Garber's concept of a "third space." Nor do all agree that the concept of transgender brings biological "sex" categories into question. For many transgendered persons, the notion of gender identity is the locus of transgender subjectivity. Feinberg portrays the relationship between the body, gender, and desire as not contingent on any "natural" factors, and as subject to change. "The transgenderist," argues Anne Bolin, ". . . disput[es] the entire concept of consistency between sexual orientation and gender" (Herdt, 485). This is precisely the "consistency" that *Stone Butch Blues* undermines. The very categories that define/confine desire —gay, straight, lesbian, bisexual—are dependent on the idea of gendered identity and biological sex. "Same-sex" desire, for example, takes on a new and paradoxical meaning if the very notion of sex is problematized.

    Stone Butch Blues portrays gender as a field of identity positions. Feinberg's position here, I think, echoes Sandy Stone's thinking on transsexual subjectivity. Stone "constitute[s] transsexuals not as a class or problematic 'third gender,' but rather as a *genre*—a set of embodied texts whose potential for *productive* disruption of structured sexualities and spectra of desire has yet to be explored" (296, italics Stone's). Although Feinberg does not portray transgendered subjects as a class, her project, and, in this chapter, mine, is to investigate the effects of class on transgender experience. In addition to the productive disruption of sex and sexuality categories Stone addresses, *Stone Butch Blues* employs a tansgendered experience to productively disrupt class divisions. Feinberg's novel interrogates a universal white masculine heterosexual subjectivity that defines itself against the bodies of those who are excluded from the category of the subject; a liberal humanist notion of individual agency; and a monolithic view of history that effaces the lived experience of working class people. It is concerned with the relationship between racism, sexism, and exclusive class structures.

    Feinberg uses the image of a continuum to describe the possibilities for gender identity. She equates "gender [with] self-expression, not anatomy" (*Transgender Liberation*, 5). The claim that gender is self-expression would seem to place Feinberg's text in the tradition of transsexual autobiography (as Jay Prosser has argued), and at odds with social constructionist gender theory. I argue, however, that although Feinberg constructs an essential self whose expression often falls within the confines of "gender," *Stone Butch Blues* clearly demonstrates that gender is a performatively constituted social construct, as is evident in the series of brutal and humiliating punishments protagonist Jess Goldberg and other transgendered characters in the novel are subject to for failing to perform gender properly. Feinberg grounds performative

theories of gender in the context of class struggle. Gender performance
emerges in *Stone Butch Blues* as a guerilla theater in which the players'
survival is at stake.

   In the epistolary opening segment, addressed to Jess's former lover
Theresa, Jess speculates on Theresa's whereabouts and imagines her
"married in another blue collar town, lying with an unemployed auto
worker who is much more like me than [university educated feminists
are]" (*Stone Butch Blues*, 11). Here, Jess identifies with the men she
works alongside in the factories and warehouses, rather than with the
middle-class feminists who exclude butch and femme lesbians from
their organizations.[8] From the novel's opening pages, then, Feinberg
focuses on class and its interrelationship with gender and sexuality.
Elsewhere in the novel, Jess identifies with butches, with members of
other oppressed groups—drag queens, the Native American women
who work in the factories, the African-American students in her high
school—and with individuals who are set apart by their difference; a
deaf mime, for example, and a homeless man who dresses in flowing
garments that de-emphasize his gender. What all of these characters
have in common, in addition to their being classified by a dominant
order as Other, is membership in the proletariat. *Stone Butch Blues* is
informed by an underlying yearning for the development of a revolutionary class consciousness among the proletariat, across gender and
racial divisions. This is precisely the yearning that some critics of the
novel have found reductive and naïve. I would like to suggest, however, that while the novel yearns for the development of class consciousness and blue-collar unity, it does not unproblematically depict the
manifestation of this consciousness or unity. In an emotionally charged
narrative segment, for example, Jess undergoes an extended period of
separation from her comrade Ed because Jess does not adequately
respond to Ed's assertions that black Americans are disproportionately
being used as cannon fodder in the Vietnam War, and because Jess
makes little effort to understand Ed's grappling with Du Boisian double
consciousness.[9] Ed commits suicide while Jess yearns for but does not
act to bring about reconciliation. In another segment, Jess's friend and
confidante, the straight white male union organizer Duffy, causes Jess
to lose her job when he inadvertently publicly identifies her as female
when she has been passing as a man in the workplace. A long period of
estrangement follows. In both of these situations there is an elemental

yearning for class unity across race or gender and sexuality boundaries, but in neither situation is this unity easily achieved, and in Jess's relationship with Ed, it is never fully achieved. Class unity, then, is presented as a limited and problematic possibility in *Stone Butch Blues*, but as a possibility worth working towards. The exploration of this possibility is one of the two primary components of the cultural work the novel performs in its focus on class issues. The second component is the limning of an oppressive pre-Stonewall past in unsparingly bold brush-strokes. Feinberg portrays in vivid and sometimes horrifying detail what Jeffrey Escoffier has termed "the political economy of the closet" (123-134). Referring to the pre-Stonewall period in lesbian and gay economic history as "the Closet Economy," Escoffier notes that "its primary economic institutions were bars, baths, adult bookstores and heavily coded mail-order services, most of which operated on the margins of legality" (123). Escoffier calls for research into the costs to gay, lesbian, and bisexual people of operating within this marginal economy while contributing to but not fully benefiting from the dominant capitalist economy, even while he notes that the actual costs will be difficult to determine and catalogue precisely because of the marginalized, encoded nature of the closet economic system. He notes that the closet economy, like the larger, dominant economic system, "has always catered more to men than to women, for reasons having to do with men's greater opportunities for employment, income, and mobility" (124). *Stone Butch Blues*, drawing on its author's personal experience and extensive research, portrays the economic (and the emotional and physical) hardships imposed on a group that existed on the margins of the already-marginalized closet economy: the transgendered.

Feinberg's purpose in writing *Stone Butch Blues* was to explore the nature of power relations and the limited possibilities for resistance outside of a supportive community, and to suggest the necessity of building an inclusive resistance.[10] The sheer force of the brutality that Jess faces on a daily basis at times overwhelms the reader. She is the grade school outcast; the junior high "lezzie" who is raped by half the football team, with the approval of the coach; and a victim of both a chilling medico-psychiatric "cure" and a well-orchestrated campaign of police terror against gender traitors—all before she is seventeen. Jess struggles alone to construct a self amid a social milieu dominated by alienation, fragmentation and loneliness. She discovers that resistance to oppression—and the refashioning of a resisting self—are lonely and losing battles outside of a resistance community. But just as the novel yearns for yet problematizes working class unity, it longs for a unified resistance among transgendered subjects even while it explores the substantial obstacles to that unity. Among these obstacles are the divergent concerns and varying levels of tolerance for transgendered self-expression linked to class status. Feinberg is primarily concerned with working-class transgendered experience, but even within this group there are considerable roadblocks to a unified resistance. *Stone Butch Blues* reiterates the danger Jess and other working-class transgendered subjects court simply by appearing together in public. The character Ruth has a "geometric theory: two people like us in public are more than double the trouble" (255). One butch or drag queen on the street is likely to be perceived as a freak and subjected to harassment; two or more together are a freak show, a traffic-stopping phenomenon, an invitation to violence. The novel introduces the questions of how, when, and whether transgendered resistance is possible, and it provides an array of answers.

The proscriptions and the violence to which Jess is constantly subjected illustrate not only the nature of daily life for those who are differently gendered, but also the variety of practices through which gender and biological sex binaries are systematically imposed upon working class bodies. When the mechanisms of gender construction are invisible—when subjects stay within the bounds of their assigned genders, gender appears to follow naturally from sex. Jess must endure almost daily violence and brutality because her expression of gender brings into full view the mechanisms that create gender, and with those mechanisms in plain view, the naturalness of gender is brought into question. As Judith Butler puts it, "we regularly punish those who fail to do their gender right" (*Gender Trouble*, 140). In the sixties and seventies, the period in which most of the novel is set, when a butch and a femme strolled down the street holding hands they suffered not only for the butch's gender treachery, but also for embodying a desire that directly challenged normative heterosexuality. Joan Nestle, a femme veteran of pre-Stonewall vice squad raids, writes that "the sight of us was enraging [to] straight spectators . . . . we were a symbol of women's erotic autonomy, a sexual accomplishment that did not include them. The physical attacks were a direct attempt to break into this self-sufficient erotic partnership" (*A Restricted Country*, 102). Upper-class cross-dressing women have always been more tolerated than working-class butch women. Nestle points out that upper-class butches like Vita Sackville-West and Radclyffe Hall have been tolerated as trendy and, I might add, reified in fashion industry imagery and constructed as icons of independence and inaccessibility in the few Hollywood films in which they appear (the defining Hollywood bourgeois butch icon is the seductive Marlene Deitrich, in the cabaret scene in *Morocco* [1930]), but working class butches have long been objects of hate, scorn, and ridicule, and they have been denigrated by feminists who have misread them as mimicking and privileging heterosexual hypermasculinity (*A Restricted Country*, 107). Middle-class feminists appear in *Stone Butch Blues* only to deny butches and femmes the opportunity to participate in the (1960s) women's liberation movement. The butches do, however, find a few allies among the men they work with, and the mostly male unions are portrayed as ignorant about transgender issues but sympathetic and inclusive of the butches. The novel yearns for class solidarity while it problematizes the gender solidarity across class divisions that existed in the rhetoric more than in the practice of Second Wave (60s and 70s) feminism.

Stone Butch Blues portrays an era in which the police systematically used sexual torture against working-class gender traitors. Butches and drag queens have historically fared the worst in vice squad raids on gay and lesbian blue-collar bars. They are the most visible gender transgressors, and in singling them out for punishment, the police attempt to inscribe both compulsory heterosexuality (since they believe that all cross-dressers are homosexual) and binary gender categories. *Stone Butch Blues* provides a detailed portrait of this process of punishment and inscription. When Jess and Ed are attacked by two policemen outside a bar, the policemen's speech reveals their thinking about gender and sexuality.

> "Eyes straight ahead," the cop behind me had his mouth close to my ear.
> The other cop began shouting at Ed. "You think you're a guy, huh? You think you can take it like a guy? We'll see. What's these?" he said. He yanked up her shirt and pulled her binder down around her waist. He grabbed her breasts so hard she gasped.
> "Leave her alone," I yelled.

"Shut up, you fuckin' pervert," the cop behind me shouted and
bashed my face against the wall. (56)

The police maintain the fiction that their victims are the predatory
ones, the "perverts." After each arrest and torture session, the butches feel alienated even from the femmes who love them. Jess dissoci-
ates from her body to dissociate from the pain and humiliation, and
she loses a bit more of her voice with each arrest, each beating. In a
singularly sickening scene a cop forces her head under water in a toilet bowl with feces floating in it. She remains passive and silent,
imagining Theresa waiting with the bail money at the booking desk
upstairs. Years later she writes to Theresa, "You prayed you wouldn't
hear me scream. I didn't" (10). "You knew it would take you weeks
again to melt the stone" (9). Elaine Scarry, writing on the relationship
between the body and discourse in state torture of prisoners, notes that
torture takes the sufferer back to "a state anterior to language" (5).
Torture translates the prisoner's pain into "a regime's fiction of power"
(18). In *Stone Butch Blues*, the police translate Jess's pain and silence
into the juridical fictions of innate gender and normative heterosexuality, the very norms she is charged with violating. Through the act of torture and the words that they speak while it is in progress, the police construct themselves as universal subjects and Jess as the excluded abject
body that validates and makes possible a universal white male heterosexual subjectivity. They also construct and reinforce class enclosures.
Upper-class lesbians in this era tended to congregate in private homes
rather than in lesbian bars, as Maxine Wolf points out; thus, working
class women were more likely to be subjected to the ritual of violence,
brutality, and humiliation that was the police raid (301-324). The police
torture literally forces Jess into a state anterior to language, but it is an
awareness of her class status that keeps Jess and the other butches silent
about the repeated acts of police brutality. They have neither the means
nor the social status (these two are of course intimately related: one
implies the other) to pursue justice or freedom from brutality. In a reiterated cycle of oppression, the butches' gender expression limits their
employment opportunities, thus placing them in economic peril and on
the margins of the working class, and their working class status makes
their gender expression doubly dangerous.

   The violent acts of oppression in *Stone Butch Blues* remain etched in
the reader's mind; the quotidian acts and proscriptions to which Jess is

subjected complete Feinberg's detailed portrait of the mechanisms of gender and class construction. Jess is harassed in and driven out of both women's and men's public restrooms, the victim of what Marjorie Garber, after Lacan, calls "urinary segregation" (13-17). Her test of passing, after the barbershop, is the public toilet. And then, of course, there is clothing. Jess chooses hers very carefully because she is more aware than are most of us of its cultural meaning. She consciously violates laws that require the wearing of three pieces of gender-specific clothing that "reflect" one's "biological" sex, preferring BVDs and an elastic binder to traditional women's underclothing, which would, to her, represent drag attire.[11] The way that Jess walks, her voice, the way she holds her body, all attract attention, because they are perceived as violating gender norms. Her dress and demeanor signify class as much as they do gender, hence she is subject to harassment due to her gender expression and the possibilities for resistance are decreased by her membership in the working class and the imposed lack of unified resistance among transgendered subjects. Jess's gender expression further complicates her position in gendered workplace relations. Passing as a man in the workplace, Jess finds that she is expected to exert male privilege and join her male co-workers in the degradation of women. When she is not passing as a man, she and other butches are not accepted as women; they are placed in a category by themselves, subjected to special taunts and humiliations, and assigned to the most dangerous and physically taxing jobs. It is the economic consequences of failing to perform gender right that Feinberg focuses on. Jess's internal monologues and conversations with confidantes reveal the most basic concerns about economic survival and restrictive class structures, not a disease with her body or her gender expression.

Feinberg provides no substantive clue as to how, when, or why Jess became differently gendered. Perhaps because Feinberg does not view Jess's gender status as an aberration she does not feel compelled to explain its origins. Gender, for Feinberg, is an expression of something that is both "always already there," and fluid. Jess says several times that she "didn't have a choice" about gender expression, that she "didn't want to be different" (13). Very early in life, Jess realizes that the problem of gender is rooted not in her body but in her culture. At age ten she thinks, "When I was really small, I thought I'd do anything to change whatever was wrong with me. Now I didn't want to change. I just wanted people to stop being mad at me all the time" (19).   She moves, then, from thinking that there is something "wrong with" her to thinking that there is something wrong with her culture. This passage effectively refutes Jay Prosser's reading of this text as a fictional trans-sexual autobiography. Prosser argues that Jess's "desire for a different body . . . has been there all along . . . at least since childhood" (495). Although *Stone Butch Blues* does share certain generic elements with transsexual autobiography, this passage makes it clear that Jess does not feel that she is trapped in the wrong body. It is not until Jess reaches working age, however, that *Stone Butch Blues* makes clear connections between Jess's relationship with her body and her position within socioeconomic structures. Or perhaps it would be more accurate to say that it is not until Jess reaches working age that she begins to question the relationship between her body, her gender, and her position within socioeconomic structures. The reader is made aware of the interrelat-edness of these constructions almost from the start of the novel. As she comes of age, Jess comes to see her body as a battleground—a site of oppression, possible resistance, and contestation.

Very early in life Jess is fashioned by dominant heterosexual culture as an abject body—an aberration against which sexual dimorphism is constructed. This construction is facilitated by her class status. Feinberg continually links Jess's gender troubles to her class status, making it clear that if Jess were a member of the middle or upper class her gender expression would doubtless have been interpreted different-ly and responded to, on a daily basis, less violently. Which is not to say that the working classes are more violent than the middle class. As a working class child, and later as an adult, Jess is more at risk of violence than are middle class gender transgressors. Few urban working class gender traitors are afforded the comparative luxury of being viewed as simply odd or eccentric. The fact that working-class butches are seen as usurpers of scarce "male" jobs, for example, compounds Jess's daily survival struggles in the workplace.

Even as a child, Jess views the social construct of gender—not her body—as a place of confinement, and confining spaces are associated in *Stone Butch Blues* with danger. The traditional symbolic association of private enclosed spaces with the feminine, warmth, receptivity, and safety is inverted. Even as a little girl, Jess gravitates toward open, public spaces. When she is about eight or nine, after a rare happy moment lying in a field and feeling as though "nature held me close and seemed to find no fault with me," Jess is attacked by a gang of boys who taunt "what are you?" (18). In a grotesque foreshadowing of her encounters with police in the years to come, the boys tie her hands behind her back, pull off her trousers, and lock her in a coal bin. She is terrified that she will never escape from the dark enclosure. "The coal was sharp and cut like knives" (18). Hours later, she is discovered, "covered with coal soot and blood, tied up and half-naked" (18). Jess's subsequent encounters with enclosed spaces signal danger. There are the public restrooms; the police vans with snarling dogs, pulled right up to the bar door during raids, leaving no escape; the police station basement interrogation/torture rooms, and the jail cells. Like the coal bin that Mrs. Jefferson, the home's occupant , must tend to herself, all of these spaces (with the exception of public bathrooms) are class enclosures; spaces rarely experienced by the rich and too-frequently experienced by Jess and other working class gender outlaws as oppressive and violent geographical manifestations of the intersection of class and gender.

The first time Jess cross-dresses in her father's suit and stands before a mirror, she is eleven years old. The suit represents not just the gendered self-expression that Feinberg claims for it, but also Jess's unconscious yearning for a class status that might afford her more breathing room as a transgendered person. Jess's moment of archetypal self-recognition is interrupted by her parents, who say nothing, but abandon her in a mental ward a few days later. This scene strikes me as out of character with the details of Jess's class identity that inform every other scene in the novel. In short, I would characterize the scene's dissonance as follows: working class transgendered people tend to be punished for failing to properly perform gender; genderqueers of more privileged classes are more likely to be subjected to cure than punishment. It seems unlikely that a child of the working class like Jess, living in a company-town ghetto, would be deposited in a mental ward. Among other questions this segment raises is the question of who pays for her hospitalization. That aside, I suspect that Feinberg may have been attempting to portray the breadth of strategies of oppression, punishment, and cure to which transgendered youth are subjected, and in so doing she violates the geography of class she has so painstakingly constructed. Jess is subjected to the "cure" generally reserved for the social

classes symbolized by the tailored suit rather than to the punishment
that more often befalls genderqueers of the working class to which she
belongs.

In the mental ward, Jess is entirely at the mercy of what Anne Bolin
calls "the privileged controllers of individual bodies, the medical pro-
fessions" (447). In the ward, Jess learns "a lot in three weeks. I real-
ized the world could do more than judge me, it wielded tremendous
power over me" (22). As oppressive as this knowledge is, she uses it to
her advantage, and pretends to go along with the psychiatric establishment's cure, which involves mandatory dress-wearing, weekly visits to
a psychiatrist, and enrollment in charm school. In the ward, she learns,
in essence, the necessity of deception. As Kate Bornstein has noted,
transgendered and transsexual people are probably the only people
encouraged by mental health practitioners to lie about their identity, to
deceive.[12] In charm school, Jess learns that she "[isn't] pretty, [isn't]
feminine, and w[ill] never be graceful" (23). What she doesn't learn,
until years later, is that her masculine gender expression is just as attractive to some women as prettiness and femininity are to some men.

Feinberg skillfully inverts notions of the naturalness of gender divisions in the novel's most macabre drag sequence and one of its most
pathetic and harrowing normative class-inscribing rituals: Butch Ro's
funeral. Ro's biological family allows the butches to attend the funeral only if they wear dresses. When Jess arrives at the funeral home,

> [t]here, around the open casket, were Butch Ro's lifelong friends.
> All of them were wearing dresses. That's how much they loved
> her. These were burly, big-shouldered he-shes who carried their
> womanhood in work-roughened hands. They could playfully
> slap you on the back and send you halfway across the room.
> Their forearms and biceps were covered with tattoos. These
> powerful butch women were comfortable in work chinos. Their
> spirit roared to life when they wore double-breasted suits.
>
> Wearing dresses was an excruciating humiliation for them.
> Many of their dresses were old, from another era when occasion-
> al retreats were still necessary. The dresses were outdated,
> white, frilly, lace, low-cut, plain. The shoes were old or bor-

rowed: patent leather, loafers, sandals. The clothing degraded
their spirit, ridiculed who they were. Yet it was in this painful
drag they were forced to say their last good-bye to the friend
they loved so much.

. . . [Butch Ro] lay in the casket . . . in a pink dress . . . holding a
bunch of pink-and-white flowers. (116-17)

Judith Butler, Marjorie Garber, and others have noted that drag has
subversive possibilities. That it foregrounds the constructedness of gender and the extent to which clothes make the man (or woman). Esther
Newton sees drag as doubly subversive, as an illusion of an illusion. In
her analysis, the drag queen presents a feminine outside (dress and
appearance) that cloaks a masculine inside (body), while simultaneously claiming a feminine inside ("essence") that is expressed on the blank
slate of the masculine outside (body) (103).[13] The reverse drag ritual at
Ro's funeral doubles this doubling and challenges the naturalness of
gender binaries. When butches dressed as butches pass as men, the
restricted categories of "men" and "women" are challenged. When
butches dressed as women cannot pass as women, the binary categories
are deconstructed altogether.

In the scene around Ro's casket, as in the opening epistolary segment
and the scenes of butch solidarity in the factories and on the loading
docks, Feinberg emphasizes class. The butches' hands are "work-
roughened," their clothes of choice are those they wear to work in the
factories, their mannerisms and gestures signify working-class identification, and their tattoos—in the era in which this novel is set—are sig-
nifiers of membership in the working classes. The dresses and shoes
they wear to the funeral are those of working class women from another era, and their class status serves to "queer" the space of the funeral
parlor even as the garments that display class attempt to conceal gender
transgression. Their class status makes them more vulnerable to the
authority imposed by the funeral home director who enforces the gender edict of Ro's family. The funeral proceeds according to Ro's family's edict until Jess and Ed, representatives of a rebellious new genera-
tion of butches, arrive wearing suits, in deliberate violation of the dress-
es-only injunction. The moment the funeral home director catches a
glimpse of Jess and Ed, he brings the viewing of Ro's body to an abrupt

halt and closes the funeral home to the butches and femmes. Jess's and Ed's transgression is two-fold; not only are they wearing "men's" clothing, they are wearing suits, which, like the suit Jess wore before the mirror as a child, signify gendered power and upper-class status. The butches, quite aware of this double signifying, buy their suits in the best men's wear stores, sparing no expense, and have them professionally tailored to fit.

The macabre drag ritual that functions to foreground class is repeated when the unemployed butches try on wigs and make-up in a desperate attempt to obtain "women's" jobs "in the department stores," since the factory jobs they had during the Vietnam war are now classified as men's work (143). "Four stone butches trying on fashion wigs," observes Jess, "It was like Halloween, only it was creepy and painful" (143). In a reversal of the moment of self-recognition before the mirror that Jess experienced when she first tried on her father's suit, she looks in the mirror at her wigged self and realizes that she "look[s] more like a he-she with a wig on than with a goddamn DA" (143). The butches abandon the wig and make-up scheme when each looks in the mirror and realizes that clothes do not make the woman. Their failed attempt at passing as made-up coifed women leads to a discussion of who they are. They recall a friend, Ginny, who began a sex-change program and is passing as Jimmy.

> Jan put her beer bottle down on the table. "Yeah, but I'm not like Jimmy. Jimmy told me he knew he was a guy even when he was little. I'm not a guy."
>
> Grant leaned forward. "How do you know that?" How do you know we aren't? We aren't real women, are we?"
>
> Edwin shook her head. "I don't know what the hell I am."
>
> I leaned over and put my arm around her shoulder. "You're my friend."
>
> Ed laughed sardonically. "Like I can really pay my rent with that." (144)

The butches demonstrate in this scene that they have internalized some of the dominant culture's gender anxiety ("We aren't real women, are we?"). They come to the uneasy conclusion that they are "he-shes," a term used derogatorily by bashers that Jess co-opts and claims as her own. For Jess, he-she means not quite a woman and not "just [a] . . . lesbian" (146). Both "he-she" and "lesbian" are laden with class value. "He-she," the term Jess becomes comfortable with, and one that is rarely heard today, was used almost exclusively by the working class, hence it is the term that Jess co-opts. Her discomfort with the word "lesbian" is referred to throughout the novel. "Lesbian," especially during the time period in which Jess's friends struggle with identity issues (the fifties and early sixties), was a middle or upper class term, when it was uttered at all, and its association with the middle and upper classes and its use by sixties and seventies feminists who denigrated butch/femme, rather than its connotations of homosexuality, account for much of Jess's distaste with the label.

Jan, Grant, Ed, and Jess question whether their problem resides in their culture's oppressive gender binaries or in their bodies. The tension between these two conflated and contested sites of oppression is a central tension in *Stone Butch Blues*. Whether the site of the problem is the body or the binary, however, all of the butches experience gender trouble most acutely (and chronically) as a problem rooted in class and economics. If their class status were other than working class, the parameters of their gender trouble would be distinctly different. I have already alluded to the fact that lesbian bars in this era often presented the sole opportunity for working class lesbians to socialize in a "safe" environment that paradoxically left customers open to the ritual abuse of the police raid. Just as they were often able to create safe social spaces in private, upper and some middle-class genderqueer women were more likely to be able to avoid abusive workplaces. Almost every episode in *Stone Butch Blues* in which a tormented butch questions her gender identity is preceded by an episode of workplace violence or humiliation, a police raid on a bar, or a violent street bashing in a working-class neighborhood. Gender dysphoria in this novel, then, is more a result of the constraints of class than it is of gender binaries or individuals' feelings that they are in the 'wrong' body.

All of the butches but Jan either have begun or are about to begin availing themselves of medically regulated technologies (hormones and surgeries, primarily) that will allow them to remake their bodies' sexed characteristics. Feinberg stresses, however, that, unlike Jimmy, whose life has been an unambiguous Female-to-Male continuum, Jan, Grant, Ed, and Jess's "problem" with their bodies is primarily an economic problem, and thus a class problem. They do not question "what the hell am I" until the answer is "unemployed." Their inability to find work, due to their gender status—not an innate discomfort with their bodies— prompts their self-questioning and gender refashioning. I must disagree, then, with Jay Prosser's assertion that "[i]t is clear that Jess's transitioning is not simply a case of butch going undercover as man out of economic necessity" (495). While I agree that Jess's case is not simple, Feinberg provides ample evidence that Jess's primary—indeed, sole—motivation for passing as a man is economic. Jess seeks stable employment and safety from violent attacks on the street and by the police. All of these are clearly class-based concerns that are greatly exacerbated by her gender *status* rather than her feelings about her gender or her body. I reiterate, however, that this is not to say that Feinberg—or this author—confers a moral judgment upon those who choose to alter their bodies' sexed characteristics for reasons other than Jess's. *Stone Butch Blues* features several characters, Jimmy and Rocco, for example, who undergo FTM transition for reasons primarily related to their discomfort with their bodies' sexed characteristics, and the text supports their choices.

The butches are acutely aware of the extent to which gender functions as a class category. As Kate Bornstein notes, "the gender binary is the one most firmly entrenched in our culture because it's the one that capitalism trades on the most, other than class" ("Puttin' On the Titz: An Entr'acte with Kate Bornstein," 17). The butches' desperation at their inability to find work underscores their double oppression: they have been assigned to the inferior biological gender category of "women," and hence denied the economic advantages that even working-class white men are privy to, and they are denied "women's work" because their gender expression is outside of the boundaries of the "women" category. *Stone Butch Blues* speaks directly to the reality of working-class butch survival and challenges the notion that butch and femme identities are mimetic of heterosexual gender roles. Feinberg also challenges the notion (here I am thinking specifically of Judith Butler) that drag is parodic. Although Jess's gender presentation contains parodic elements, Feinberg, like Joan Nestle, describes it as primarily expressive of something that is "always already there"—in distinct opposition to artificially constructed social class.

Jess, Grant, and the other butches repeatedly frame their identity issues in the language of geography. With this language of place, Feinberg employs a class-based conceit. One's place, one's sense of belonging, is inextricably bound to one's class status. The bars, the workplaces, and the community in which Jess moves are distinctly working class, and class constraints prevent Jess from seeking community elsewhere. Conversely, while Jess feels shut out of everything and everywhere, she also feels trapped: "I don't feel like a man trapped in a woman's body, I just feel trapped" (158-59). The butches are trapped in an endless cycle of temporary jobs and economic dependence on their femmes, who enjoy relative job stability in traditionally female occupations such as clerical work and prostitution. The butches feel that they've got "no place to hide" (159). Socioeconomic currents and constant punishment for gender transgression drives Jess to a resistance strategy that, for her, ultimately proves unworkable: she makes the difficult decision to begin hormone treatments and pass as a man.

As a man, Jess lives in fear of discovery and finds that she has to invent a new history and identity to match her new hormonally-altered body. With her breasts in a binder and beard stubble on her face, Jess cannot even engage in a social activity as simple as going to the gym for a steambath and a swim with the guys from work. To complete her identity change, Jess has breast reduction surgery. Even while the medical establishment is in the process of shaping her body to fit into an accepted gender category, it reminds Jess that she is a transgressor, a monster. She is thrown out of the hospital before she has even recovered from the effects of the anesthesia, let alone those of the surgery, because "this hospital is for sick people," not freaks (177). Compared with the reinforcement that the medical establishment gives women who opt for breast "augmentation" surgery—the after-effects of which are now known to be ruinous to women's health—the treatment that Jess receives is particularly illuminative of the nature of the medical processes of "biological" gender construction.

Jess cannot obtain identification documents that match her appearance; with the *"f."* box checked on her driver's license, even a routine traffic stop by police could result in discovery and punishment. She feels as constrained by her new body and identity as she did in her former one: "A feeling of claustrophobia choked me. Even as my world was expanding, it was shrinking" (175). She is forced to concede that, for her, the psychological and social disadvantages of passing as a man outweigh the economic advantages—the primary one being the availability of steady work.

Jess simultaneously begins to experience a measure of comfort in her new body and an isolation unlike any that she has known. Here the tension between the body as the site of oppression and as the locus of resistance reaches its zenith. Jess has altered her body as a strategy of resistance, and the strategy at first appears to have worked: she finds stable employment and she finds herself free from gender oppression for the first time in her life. But her new body is not the locus of resistance she envisioned. Rather, she experiences it as a symbol of victory for the forces that punished her for failing to properly perform gender. The binary vision of the outside world constructed Jess as a "man trapped in a woman's body," and she has now altered her body to conform to this diagnosis.[14] Although passing has its pluses, Jess still feels that there is "no place outside of me where I [belong]" (209). She has modified her body as a way of dealing with economic hardship (unemployment) and harassment, but it remains clear that the external surface of her body does not dictate who she is. She is comfortable in the space outside of gender binaries, but the world continually tries to roust her from that space, and to keep her firmly constrained by class divisions.

In her new body, Jess assumes that no lesbian femme would accept her as a lover, and even if one would, there is no longer a community or a meeting place to facilitate such a connection. She is both attracted to and terrified by straight women. Finally, the attraction and loneliness get the better of her terror, and she ends up in bed with Annie, a working-class straight homophobic woman who thinks Jess is a man. In this scene, Feinberg weaves a complex symbolic narrative in which class is as cogently signified as gender. Through sleight of hand and skillful manipulation of a dildo, Jess lives up to—and exceeds—Annie's expectations. Annie is clearly impressed by Jess's skill as a lover and by the fact that their lovemaking focuses on Annie's, not Jess's, pleasure. "'You don't fuck like other guys,'" she says, "'It's like you got a brain in your dick instead of a dick for a brain" (193). When my students read *Stone Butch Blues* last year, they found Jess to be a very likable character and they were angered at the injustices to which she was subjected, but they found the scene with Annie to be utterly unbelievable. I found it to be unlikely, but certainly not unbelievable. Marjorie Garber observes—and documents—that the sort of performance enacted by Jess and Annie has been enacted "dozens, probably hundreds" of times in recent history, for time periods often spanning the participants' entire lives (67). Brandon Teena, a young, biologically (unaltered) female transgendered (FTM) person who was murdered for his gender transgressions in Falls City, Nebraska in 1993, was described by five of his former partners, all of whom identified as heterosexual women, as "the best boyfriend they had ever dated, the most alluring suitor and certainly the best lover" (24).[15] None of them thought of themselves as lesbians or of Teena as a woman. What my students found difficult to believe is precisely what Annie, and Brandon Teena's partners, found so satisfying about the encounter: the notion of heterosexual sex that is not penis-centered, that is focused on the woman's body. The scene's irony, of course, is derived from the fact that both of the participants are women (Jess never ceases to think of herself as a woman, even when she is passing). Feinberg effectively deconstructs, in this scene, both the naturalness of maleness, and hence its claims to universal subjectivity, and the authenticity of the penis, which is precisely, I think, why some of my students found the scene challenging. Where there is a penis present, male privilege asserts that it will be the center of attention, and Feinberg decenters that expectation. David Henry Hwang, in an interview focusing on his play *M. Butterfly*, addresses—and supports—the expectation of the centrality of the penis. In a discussion of "male frontal nudity" in the play, and his decision to downplay it, to have the nude actor stand downstage and at an angle to the audience, he asserts, with authority, that "... if you have a penis here and Sir Laurence Olivier there, everybody looks at the penis" (152). In the scene with Annie and Jess, the "penis" is there, and the reader's—and Annie's—attention is riveted on Sir Lawrence Olivier.

But the phallus here is not simply representative of masculine power; it is an object with a long history and, more recently, a signifier of class. Colleen Lamos writes that "the dildo has circulated within popular culture, satiric tales, and subliterary, pornographic genres in the West since at least the seventeenth century. The use of dildos has been proscribed in various ecclesiastical codes, while commercial possession of dildos is illegal in some states," including Texas, (101).

Performance artist Jim Rose was recently arrested for appearing on stage in Lubbock, Texas, fully clothed, wearing a strap-on dildo. Possession of six or more dildos in Texas makes one liable to prosecution for "intent to promote" their use. Lamos argues that cultural anxiety about the dildo arises from an unconscious understanding that "the dildo both imitates and undercuts the phallicism of the penis, discrediting phallic power while simultaneously, and paradoxically, assuming such power for itself" (102) and that as "[a] detachable part, the dildo humorously implies that the penis can be detached from its phallic burden—or that the phallus has spawned another symbol. Like simulacra in general, it is threatening and alluring in different contexts as a substitutive displacement of that which it represents" (120). Both of Lamos's readings of the dildo are born out in the scene with Annie. The power of the phallus is undercut by the focus on Annie's pleasure, and by the reader's understanding that the "penis" in this scene lacks both sensation and naturalness. The humorous implications of the dildo are multilayered: Annie thinks the joke is on "other" men who have not been as skilled at the art of lovemaking as Jess; the joke is on Annie, who thinks Jess is a man and believes that homosexuals are child-molesting perverts; and the phallus is indeed detachable. But the dildo also functions as a reviled class signifier. Again, I cite Lamos:

> . . . the dildo was decried by many lesbian feminists in the 1970s and 1980s as a straight male fantasy, a myth contrived by jealous men who could not imagine two women sexually satisfying each other, or else disavowed as a retrograde, male-identified practice stemming from false consciousness or penis envy. Like the butch lesbian, it was relegated to the benighted, prefeminist past, the product of outdated notions of sexual inversion. (104)

The charge of "false consciousness" to which Lamos refers was often leveled at working class women, and at working class lesbians in particular, and, to lesbian feminists, the dildo was a primary signifier of that "false" consciousness. Dorothy Allison writes that although "[i]n 1979, the idea of using dildos was still anathema to most feminist lesbians," lesbians were furtively using them, and feminist lesbians were being schooled in their use by their working-class lovers, where such liaisons across class boundaries existed (132). *Stone Butch Blues* vividly sketches the treatment of working class butch and femme lesbians by feminists active in the Second Wave women's movement. In foregrounding the dildo in the Annie segment, and elsewhere in the novel—Jess's first symbolic point of transition from "baby butch" to adult occurs when an older butch presents her with a dildo; a later significant moment in her development involves a femme telling her what it signifies to femmes and how she is to use it—Feinberg implicitly foregrounds class and the class divisions the Second Wave women's movement effaced.

Although the bedroom scene with Annie appears to invite a reading of Jess's body as a site of resistance—to universal white masculine subjectivity and the "naturalness" of gendered and sexed bodies—the narrative encourages another reading. Shortly after the one-night stand with Annie, Jess reaches a crisis point of isolation and alienation. She reconnects with Edna, an old femme friend, and, again employing a negative spatial trope, confesses that she feels "'[l]ike [she has] been buried alive'" (213) in her own body. Rather than confirming her identity, passing as a man has fragmented it. Before passing, she claims, she knew who she was: a he-she. Now she is not sure. "I don't know what I am," she tells Edna. In using "what" and not "who," Jess questions her humanity. She adopts the language of her enemies, of those who used to call her "it" before she passed. She now sees herself as a negative, as "neither" a man nor a woman, and she "'[doesn't] like being neither'" (218). Edna responds that Jess is "'more than just neither. There's other ways to be'" (218). Again, Jess squares off against her fragmented self in the mirror, the syringe of hormones poised above her thigh. This time she realizes,

> As much as I loved my beard as part of my body. I felt trapped behind it. What I saw reflected in the mirror was not a man, but I couldn't recognize the he-she. . . . I could see my passing self, but even I could no longer see the more complicated me beneath my surface. . . . I hadn't just believed that passing would hide me. I hoped that it would allow me to express the part of myself that didn't seem to be a woman. I didn't get to explore being a he-she, though. I simply became a he—a man without a past. (222)

The only time Jess feels trapped in the wrong body, then, is when she is passing as a man. This scene foregrounds Feinberg's expressive hypothesis. Motivated by economic necessity, Jess's performance as a man is parodic and unfulfilling. Feinberg privileges the expression of a self outside of gender, not the subversive performance of gender. It is implied that Jess will achieve fulfillment only when the performance of gender and the expression of self coincide. The constraints of class are the primary obstacle to this desired intersection of "self" and gender. If Jess did not have to worry constantly about getting or keeping a job and about living hand to mouth, the cusp of gender and self would be more accessible to her; she could be the eccentric, the dandy in a suit, the maiden aunt. None of these identities are accessible to the working class butches in *Stone Butch Blues*.

The half-formed yearning for a past, a history, that has crept into Jess's consciousness throughout the narrative comes to the fore in the scene before the mirror with the syringe, and it stays Jess's hand from injecting the hormones. The postmodern Jess, the man without a history, is erased and the he-she resurfaces. Jess begins to see her body as a possible site of resistance, and this time the thought does not isolate or exhaust as much as it empowers. In the final pages of the novel Feinberg provides closure by suggesting that the gendered body may productively be seen as a site of both oppression and resistance only when the inseparability of class, gender, and sexuality issues is acknowledged and analyzed.

A growing consciousness of the historical and socioeconomic context of her struggles enables Jess to envision her body as a locus of resistance and facilitates her understanding of the relationship of social class to gender expression. Even before history becomes important to Jess, *Stone Butch Blues* is infused with it. The novel interweaves snippets and narratives from labor history, the Civil Rights struggle, anti-Vietnam War activism, Wounded Knee, and the women's movement. All of these historic struggles are situated within the context of class struggle. Each of these historic movements is seen in terms of the deep fractures it brings about in Jess's high school, in the butch-femme community, and among assembly-line workers. Each is evaluated in terms of its support or subversion of class hierarchies. Finally, Jess becomes a public activist, and Feinberg suggests that the labor and gay liberation movements of the nineties possess the potential to subvert class structures. The novel closes with Jess yearning for and working towards a conflation of organized labor and gay liberation struggle, apparently articulating Feiniberg's belief that such a conflation is possible and desirable. Given the nature of the novel's unrelenting portrayal of the quotidian brutalities that function to construct gender and to keep gender transgressors in their place, the ending seems almost utopian. But it is an ending that reflects the novel's time and its timeliness. The United States does not appear to be witnessing a revival of popular support for organized labor; however, both the gay civil rights struggle of the nineties and queer studies at the fin de millénaire are beginning to address class and transgender issues.

Jess finds her voice and a language in which to express herself when she happens upon a gay liberation rally in the street. It is not the first such rally she has seen, but in the past she has "always walked away feeling outside of that movement and alone," no doubt because she associates it with her rejection by white middle class feminists in the women's movement (296). This time, however, she hears a young woman testifying before a large crowd about having been raped by a gang of young men from her neighborhood. She was raped because she was singled out as a lesbian. "'I never told my lover what happened,'" the woman concludes, "'I felt like we'd have both been raped if I told her'" (296). The story strikes a familiar chord for Jess. Ironically, it is another woman's testimony to silence that moves Jess to public speech, that makes her feel "so sick to death of my own silence that I needed to speak too" (296). Dizzy with fear, Jess mounts the stage.

> I'm not a gay man. I'm a butch, a he-she. I don't know if the people who hate our guts call us that anymore. But that single epithet shaped my teenage years. . . . I watch protests and rallies from across the street. . . . There's lots of us who are on the outside, and we don't want to be. We're getting busted and beaten up. We're dying out here. We need you—but you need us too.(296)

In claiming a voice and a history, Jess inserts her body—the transgendered body—into resistance strategy. The tension between the body as the site of oppression and as the locus of resistance appears to be almost too easily resolved. She acknowledges that her body has been a site of oppression, and she simultaneously claims it as a site of resistance. Her

first two sentences respond to the misreading of her body she anticipates receiving from the crowd. She asserts what Leslie Adelson asserts
in making a claim for the importance of real bodies to resistance history: that the body "is both within and outside the reach of dominant
orders [and] resistance to oppression is a matter not of missing heroes
beyond the invisible walls of culture but of everyday mortals: you and
me . . ." (34-35). Feinberg would stress the "and" in Adelson's "you and
me." In asserting "There's lots of us who are on the outside, and we
don't want to be," it is clear that Jess is not speaking about sexuality—
she is, after all, addressing an audience at a gay liberation rally. The
"us" on the outside, "getting busted and beaten up," are transgendered
subjects who will not get a foot in the door of the gay liberation movement for another decade or so past the point at which Jess makes her
speech; "us" also refers to the working class that the movement of the
seventies, eighties, and most of the nineties has effaced. Feinberg's
project then, is not just about delineating the effect of class constraints
on gender expression and construction; it is about suggesting the necessity of opening up gay civil rights struggle to class analysis and transgender issues. *Stone Butch Blues*, published on the eve of an era in
which "gay marriage" has, for better or worse, become synonymous
with gay civil rights, perhaps anticipates the significance of gender
issues (such as the far-reaching implications of defining marriage as a
legal tie 'between one man and one woman') to gay civil rights struggle.

In the purview of this novel, transgender issues are working class
issues. This has been the case, for the most part, with nascent transgender liberation struggles. Speaking to her labor organizer friend
Duffy in the novel's final pages, Jess confirms

> Something incredible happened to me today, Duffy." I got up in front
> of a rally and talked over a microphone. I wanted to tell them how it
> was in the plants, how when a contract's almost up management works
> overtime trying to divide everybody. I didn't know if they'd get what
> I meant if I said it takes the whole membership to win a strike. (299)

In Feinberg's assessment, meaningful resistance can only take place
when there is a revolutionary working class consciousness, and the
yearning for this consciousness that has marked every page of the novel

becomes more pronounced at its close. Jess has progressed from enacting a modernist individual agency that brought isolation, exclusion, and alienation, to working as a resisting subject within existing structures—labor unions and the nascent gay and lesbian liberation movement. The final pages leave us with the promise of Jess working with others to create a space for the transgendered subject and for the address of class and gender issues within both of these organized resistance structures. Her presence in the labor movement necessitates an examination of the movement's treatment of gender and of women, and her presence as a working-class butch in the gay liberation movement underscores the class issues the movement has been slow to address. Jess's understanding of herself as an individual agent wanes as the narrative progresses and she becomes aware of historic resistance struggles. *Stone Butch Blues* ultimately emphasizes collective action and coalition-building as tactics of resistance. It examines the relationship between gender and class structures, and it suggests means by which such an examination might advance a praxis of resistance.

Notes

1. Garber envisions a "'third' . . . space of possibility . . . which questions binary thinking." She emphasizes that this "third" is "not . . . a *sex*, certainly not an instantiated 'blurred' sex as signified by a term like `androgyne' or `hermaphrodite' . . . The `third' is a mode of articulation, a way of describing . . ." (italics in original).

2 It is nearly impossible, for example, to work in gender theory today and not address the work of Judith Butler; yet Butler, and most of her contemporaries, are all but silent on issues of social class. Butler's crucial concepts of performativity and abject bodies tend to reduce complex social milieu to insider/outsider dichotomies such as hetero/homo, empowered/disempowered, and, occasionally, universal white male subjectivity/women of color. Butler's work is clearly groundbreaking and has been deservedly influential, but, like much contemporary work that theorizes gender, it invites a closer examination of the complex interrelationship of gender, transgender, and class issues; the issues

this chapter sets out to explore. See, for example, Butler's treatment, in *Bodies that Matter* of Jennie Livingston's *Paris is Burning* ("Gender is Burning," 121-140). Butler acknowledges the significance of class and race in the film but then proceeds to discuss it in terms that illuminate her ideas about performativity and abject bodies but do not interrogate its treatment of class and race.

3. *Stone Butch Blues* won the American Library Association's 1993 award for best gay or lesbian novel.

4. Leslie Martin Lothstein's *Female-to-Male Transsexualism* (1983) was the only book-length study, prior to 1996, to address the female-to-male subject, and Lothstein's perspective is clinical. He regards transsexualism as "a disorder of the self." Marjorie Garber laments the invisibility and critical misunderstanding of the female-to-male (FTM) transgendered subject. She goes a long way toward exposing and correcting this misunderstanding, in *Vested Interests*, and argues that FTM cross-dressers and transsexuals have been ignored because MTF expression is seen—especially by the medical establishment—as a curable psychosis (the cure being sex-reassignment surgery), and FTM expression is seen as a simple desire to *be* a man, a desire that the medical-psychiatric establishment has long believed that all women develop and, in "normal" development, repress and subjugate (x). FTMs are now beginning to speak for themselves, on the internet, through small presses, and through organizations like Transexual [sic] Menace. Several new books on the subject were due out as this book went to press.

5. Gender Identity Disorder appears in the American Psychiatric Association's *Diagnostic and Statistical Manual of Mental Disorders*. Gender dysphoria is defined by the medico-psychiatric system in terms of the "patient" being "trapped in the wrong body," a man trapped in a woman's body or vice versa. Sandy Stone points out that the medico-psychiatric system that invented Gender Identity Disorder denies sex reassignment surgery to individuals who do not state that they feel "trapped in the wrong body," and that persons desiring surgery are therefore compelled to state that they feel trapped in the wrong body, whether they do or not; that the medico-psychiatric text quite literally *creates* the pre-operative transsexual subject who feels trapped in the wrong body. Recently, there has been considerable debate in transgender communities about the wisdom of demanding a removal of Gender Identity Disorder from the American Psychiatric Association's *Diagnostic and Statistical Manual of Mental Disorders*. Some community member feel that its removal would expedite transgender liberation; others fear that the removal of the classification would make it more difficult or impossible to secure health insurance coverage of sex reassignment procedures.

6.   I do not mean to imply that Feinberg argues—or that I argue—that *no* individual is gender dysphoric or that individuals should not have access to medical technologies for altering the body's sexed characteristics—technologies currently accessible primarily to those have been diagnosed with gender identity disorder. Feinberg argues that these options should be readily accessible to those who desire them.   I argue that her protagonist, although she does employ some sex reassignment technologies, is driven to do so primarily by socioeconomic concerns and class constraints, not by gender dysphoria.

7.   Butler, Garber, Kate Bornstein, Martine Rothblatt, and others argue that biological sex is as problematic a category as gender.   They point out that traditional biological markers of sex self-deconstruct under scrutiny, as does the "science" that invented them.   Rothblatt, for example, observes that "it is not true that all legally defined women are XX and all legally defined men are XY [chromosomally].   Hundreds of thousands of people are born with all manner of chromosomal variations, including XXY and X, among others.   The Olympics has ceased using chromosomal tests for a second X as a means of disqualifying women, after certain athletes—namely persons with a vagina, a lifelong "female" gender identity, and but one X chromosome—were cruelly disqualified right at the quadrennial event" (6).   I address Bornstein's work below.

8.   Gendered pronouns become problematic here.   The English language has not yet caught up with the transgender revolution.   To avoid confusion, I will use gender-specific pronouns—and the noun "woman"—as Feinberg uses them.   Feinberg refers to her protagonist as both a woman and a "he-she."   I refer to Jess throughout as "she" because, although she chooses to pass as a man for a time, she never refers to herself as a man, and she presents herself to those with whom she is intimate as a woman or a "he-she."   Her confidantes and allies use the pronoun "she" to refer to Jess.

9.   Ed loans Jess a copy of W. E. B. Du Bois's 1903, *The Souls of Black Folk*, with the following passage from the essay "Of Our Spiritual Strivings" marked (178): "It is a peculiar sensation, this double consciousness, this sense of always looking at oneself through the eyes of others, of measuring one's soul by the tape of a world that looks on in amused contempt and pity.   One ever feels his twoness—an American, a Negro; two souls, two thoughts, two unreconciled strivings, two warring ideals in one dark body, whose dogged strength alone keeps it from being torn asunder."

10.   Feinberg outlined this rhetorical purpose in the question and answer session following a speech on 11 April, 1994, closing Penn State University's (University Park, PA) Lesbian, Gay, and Bisexual Pride Week.

11. In an autobiographical segment of *Transgender Warriors*, Feinberg writes that three-pieces-of gender-specific-clothing laws were on the books and were regularly and brutally enforced in Buffalo in the early sixties (8).

12. Bornstein made this observation during a discussion with the audience after a 1994 performance of *The Opposite Sex is Neither* at Penn State. She was referring to the fact that the medical/psychiatric establishment counsels sex-change patients, pre- and post-operative, not to identify as transgendered or transsexual, but to pass as the gender they are encouraged to think of themselves as in the process of "becoming."

13. The majority of discourse on drag to date has focused on the male-to-female (MTF) cross-dresser and transsexual. Marjorie Garber addresses (FTM) cross-dressing in *Vested Interests*.

14. I wish to reiterate that Jess's interpretation of her hormonally and sur-gically altered body as a symbol of victory for the forces of gender oppression reflects her understanding of her body and her culture. Neither Jess, Feinberg, nor I argue that transgendered persons' use of medical technologies to alter their bodies is *always* the wrong choice or a victory for gender conservatism. Feinberg has stated, and I concur, that access to medical technologies for re-embodiment should be a right and a choice, not an imposition or, as is the case with Jess, an economic necessity.

15. Minkowitz insists on referring to Teena as a lesbian woman, although Teena clearly refused both of those appellations and identified as a heterosexu-al male. Many transgendered people and other *Village Voice* readers took offense at Minkowitz's refusal to honor Teena's choices.

Afterword

"Sabotage and Subversion, then, are this Book's Objectives"

> Sabotage and subversion, then, are this book's objectives.
> Go, my book, and help destroy the world as it is.
>
> —Penultimate sentence of Russell Banks's *Continental Drift.*

This book began with the notion that an exploration of the relationship between identity, subjectivity, and agency in dissenting fictions would reveal a viable subjectivity from which a resisting agency could be enacted. My aim was to uncover the theory as it existed in praxis in dissenting fictions; to elucidate the mechanisms through which a viable subjectivity—a site from which resistance tactics and strategies can be enacted—is constituted in dissenting fictions.

In closing, I would like to outline the key strategies and tactics that make subjectivity viable and resistance possible in dissenting fictions. Chief among these is the assumption that the idea of the subject is dependent on social structures (race, class, gender) and institutions, but that it is not produced by those structures and institutions in a predictable hierarchical power relationship. The distinction I make, in other words, is a distinction between a structured subject and a subject that interacts with structures. The liberal humanist notion of subjectivity that constrains Bob Dubois, for example, is a social construct—a structure—that has been envisioned as a pre-existing entity that is located outside of or *against* structures such as other subjects, nature, and society. Dissenting fictions reject this vision of the subject and its limited possibilities for resistance. They envision instead a subject that interacts with (social, linguistic, institutional, juridical, political, etc.) structures in what Butler calls a reiterative citational relationship. Through this relationship, the subject is reiteratively identified in relation to structures, but the possibility exists for repeating identity codes with a *difference*. And it is not just a possibility. The dissenting subject moves from possible to actual resistance, interacting with other subjects to create what Burnham calls "loopholes of retreat" within culturally constructed structures.

In *Stone Butch Blues*, for example, Jess is reiteratively constituted by various mouthpieces for social structures as a "girl," a "woman," a "freak," and a "cute man." She rejects all of these identities and reiterates instead, in her words and actions, a "he-she" identity, co-opting the language of oppressive structures and reinventing herself as a dissenting subject. In *Jazz*, Violet is reiteratively constituted in negative terms, as "not-white," "not light," and "not-young." After initially internalizing these negatives, and developing a fragmented identity as a result, she engages with the structures she has both internalized and attempted to isolate herself from, recognizing the interactive relationship between subject and structure: "What's the world for if you can't make it up the way you want it? . . . If you don't, it will change you and it'll be your fault cause you let it" (208). She reinvents herself as "the woman . . . I used to like before . . ." (208).

It is crucial to note, however, that Violet and Jess do not reinvent themselves through individual relations of power and discourse. They—and dissenting subjects in general—move beyond social constructionism to a practice of interpersonal engaged agency, to an awareness of the relationship of social structures to agency. Subjects who see themselves as individual, isolated actors—Bob Dubois, for example, or Violet and Joe Trace in the early segments of *Jazz*, or Menardo in the *Almanac*, are failed subjects in dissenting fictions. Given the increasing instability of identity categories, these novels construct resisting agency as necessarily interactive, with a focus on actions, on agency, rather than on individual identities.

Dissenting fictions focus on community, on coalition-building, and on the necessity of human interaction. In their emphasis on commonalities, however, they do not efface difference. They emphasize the interrelatedness of components of identity. Bradley's Adlai Stevenson Brown, for example, comes to an understanding of the inseparability of race, class, and gender issues. Silko's characters build a network of multicultural resistance communities, but they stress a respect for difference. Bradley and Silko explore class as a unifying factor in resistance movement. Neither author finds class unity to be unproblematic or universal, perhaps because they are looking for points of commonality rather than universal unifying factors. Both writers, however, find class to be a potentially unifying category, if not an uncomplicated one.

In locating points of commonality, dissenting fictions focus on what Foucault has termed local and specific points of resistance. Their coalitions and networks grow out of the intimate and personal and toward the global. They employ narratives of intimate interpersonal relations to address relations of oppression and resistance on a larger social scale, as Silko does with the Monte kidnapping narrative and Banks does with Bob's working-class frustration and Vanise's Middle Passage to America. Dissenting fictions rework the 1960s assertion that the personal is political, adding the injunction that the personal is not just personal, it is interpersonal and engaged with social structures.

These fictions claim subjectivity and engaged interactive agency for the dissenting subject through the mechanism of the recovery of history. They present alternative histories that deploy an array of resistance strategies. The resistance strategies I have laid out do not constitute a unified theory, but they are unified in their debt to resistance history.

Dissenting fictions simultaneously decenter and foreground actual historical events by focussing not on the event itself but on its aftermath; its effects on individual lives and the lives of families, tribes, and communities years and miles removed from the event. Morrison uses this technique in *Jazz* with both the Great Migration North and the silent march down Fifth Avenue. Feinberg both foregrounds and decenters the Stonewall rebellion by writing it into her characters' lives as an inspiration and the birth of a movement while never actually describing the event that was Stonewall. It is reported secondhand, in a brief sentence. Feinberg foregrounds the fact that small Stonewalls occurred weekly in the butch-femme and drag queen communities, and that their heroes, as in the case of history's Stonewall, were everyday working-class transgendered people. Resistance to oppression is made possible in dissenting fictions, then, through the construction of history as the story of everyday embodied subjects acting in solidarity with other embodied subjects.

Dissenting Fictions present polyvocal perspectives on history that function to empower marginalized subjects rather than to present competing and cancelling narrative "truths." In offering multiple resistance histories, they multiply sites of resistance. The *Almanac of the Dead* and *The Chaneysville Incident* focus on the role of discourse in resistance practice, but other dissenting fictions address this concern as well. *Jazz*'s narrator, in the novel's final segment, considers the role of discourse in the construction of subjectivity. Jess Goldberg steps up to the podium at the gay liberation rally not only to empower herself but to become part of a resistance community.

In enacting a resisting subjectivity at the podium, Jess stresses the corporeality of subjectivity, the relationship between identity, resistance, and the body. Dissenting fictions address the tension between notions of the body as the locus of oppression and as the site of resisting subjectivity. They reject what Susan Bordo calls the postmodern conception of the body as cultural plastic. Rather than attempting to alter the body—or after discovering, as Jess and Violet do, that neither the process nor the results of altering the body are simple or satisfying—they challenge the notion that the body, rather than the culture that constructs it—is the locus of dis-ease. Dissenting fictions address the means by which (Butler's) "abject" or "unthinkable" bodies—the bodies of those excluded from the category of the subject—function to "circumscribe the zone of the subject" (Butler, *Bodies that Matter* 3). Russell Banks asserts that Bob is reiteratively constituted as a universal subject in his movement toward and retreat from the body of the excluded Other. Golden Gray embraces, and in embracing becomes the unthinkable abject body. Gray's narrative functions metaphorically to demonstrate that the "abjected outside"—what Morrison, in *Playing in the Dark*, calls the "not-me"—functions as the "founding repudiation" of subjectivity (Butler, *Bodies that Matter* 3).

Dissenting fictions insert the body, the embodied interactive agent, into resistance history. History, in these novels, is experienced by living bodies, enacted by embodied subjects. The establishment of the body as the site of oppression, as the site of reiterated citational practices, does not preclude its functioning as the site of resistance. On the contrary, the fact that the body is a locus of oppression necessitates its functioning as a site of resistance: in Foucauldian terms, where there is power there is resistance. The body, in dissenting fictions, functions as a local and specific point of resistance. Jess, for example, resists gender oppression by responding to the reiterative citational practice that identifies her body as abject, as the locus of freak-ness, by reiterating an embodied he-she identity and rejecting gender binaries.

Dissenting fictions reject other binaries as well: masculine/feminine, old/young, essence/social construction, straight/gay, and body/mind, to name a few. These novels present diverse variety of strategies united in their insistence on an embodied dissenting subject, an engaged interpersonal concept of agency, and the recovery of resistance history.

Works Cited

Primary Works

Banks, Russell. *Continental Drift*. New York: Ballantine, 1985.

Bradley, David. *The Chaneysville Incident*. 1981. New York: Harper, 1990.

——. *South Street*. New York: Grossman, 1975.

Ellison, Ralph. *Invisible Man*. New York: Random, 1952.

Faulkner, William. *The Sound and the Fury*. 1929. New York: Random, 1954.

Feinberg, Leslie. *Stone Butch Blues*. Ithaca: Firebrand, 1993.

——. "Butch to Butch: A Love Song." Nestle, *The Persistent Desire* 80-94.

Morrison, Toni. *Beloved*. 1987. New York: NAL, 1988.

——. *The Bluest Eye*. 1970. New York: Pocket: 1972.

——. *Jazz*. New York: Knopf, 1992.

——. *Song of Solomon*. 1977. New York: NAL, 1978.

——. *Tar Baby*. 1981. New York: NAL, 1983.

——. *Sula*. 1973. New York: Penguin, 1982.

Silko, Leslie Marmon. *Almanac of the Dead*. New York: Simon, 1991.

——. Ceremony. 1977. New York: Penguin, 1986.

Secondary Works

Adelson, Leslie. *Making Bodies, Making History: Feminism and German Identity*. Lincoln: U of Nebraska P, 1993.

Alcoff, Linda. "Cultural Feminism versus Poststructuralism: The Identity Crisis in Feminist Theory." *Signs* 13.3 (1988): 405-36.

Allen, Paula Gunn. *The Sacred Hoop: Recovering the Feminine in American Indian Traditions.* Boston: Beacon, 1986, 1992.

Allison, Dorothy. *Skin: Talking About Sex, Class, and Literature.* Ithaca: Firebrand, 1994.

Appiah, Anthony. "Tolerable Falsehoods: Agency and the Interests of Theory." *Consequences of Theory.* Ed. Jonathan Arac and Barbara Johnson. Baltimore: Johns Hopkins UP, 1991. 63-90.

Arac, Jonathan, ed. *After Foucault: Humanistic Knowledge, Postmodern Challenges.* New Brunswick: Rutgers UP, 1988.

Banks, Russell. "The Search for Clarity: An Interview With Russell Banks." Trish Reeves. *New Letters.* 53.3 (1987): 44-59.

Bawer, Bruce. "All that Jazz." Rev. of Jazz, by Toni Morrison. *The New Criterion.* May 1992: 10-17.

Bell, Bernard. *The Afro-American Novel and Its Tradition.* Amherst: U of Massachusetts P, 1987.

Boas Franz. *Keresan Texts.* Vol. 1. Publications of the American Ethnological Society 8. 1928. 2 vols; rpt. New York: AMS, 1974.

Bolin, Anne. "Transcending and Transgendering: Male-to-Female Transsexuals, Dichotomy and Diversity." Herdt 447-486.

Bordo, Susan. *Unbearable Weight: Feminism, Western Culture, and the Body.* Berkeley: U of California P, 1993.

Bornstein, Kate. Forum on "Transgender Politics," sponsored by the PSU Lesbian, Gay, and Bisexual Student Alliance. The Pennsylvania State University, 8 April 1995.

——. *Gender Outlaw.* New York: Routledge, 1994.

——. "Puttin' On the Titz: An Entr'acte with Kate Bornstein." Trish Thomas. *Mondo 2000* 13 (Dec. 1994): 114-117.

Bradley, David. "The Business of Writing: An Interview with David Bradley." With Susan Blake and James A. Miller. *Callaloo: An African-American and African Journal of Arts and Letters* 7.2 (1984): 19-39.

——. "Telling the Black Woman's Story." *New York Times Magazine,* January, 1984. 34.

Brantlinger, Patrick. "Victorians and Africans: The Genealogy of the Myth of the Dark Continent." *Critical Inquiry* 12 (1985): 166.

Burnham, Michelle. "Loopholes of Resistance: Harriet Jacobs' Slave Narrative and the Critique of Agency in Foucault." *Arizona Quarterly* 49.2 (1993): 53-73.

Butler, Judith. *Bodies that Matter: On the Discursive Limits of "Sex."* New York: Routledge, 1993.

——. *Gender Trouble: Feminism and the Subversion of Identity.* New York: Routledge, 1990.

Castillo, Susan Perez. "Postmodernism, Native American Literature and the Real: The Silko-Erdrich Controversy." *Massachusetts Review* 32 (1991): 285-94.

Christian, Barbara. "Community and Nature in the Novels of Toni Morrison. *The Journal of Ethnic Studies* 7.4 (1980): 65-78.

Churchill, Ward, ed. *Marxism and Native Americans.* Boston: South End, n.d.

Cixous, Hélène. "The Laugh of the Medusa." Trans. Keith Cohen and Paula Cohen. *Signs* 1.4 (Summer 1976). Rpt. in *New French Feminisms.* Ed. Elaine Marks and Isabelle de Courtivron. New York: Schocken, 1981. 245-264.

——. "Sorties: Out and Out: Attacks/Ways Out/Forays." *The Newly Born Woman.* Hélène Cixous and Catherine Clement. Trans. Betsy Wing. Minneapolis: U of Minnesota P, 1986. 63-132.

Clatterbaugh, Kenneth. *Contemporary Perspectives on Masculinity.* Boulder: Westview, 1990.

Davis, Cynthia. "Self, Society, and Myth in Toni Morrison's Fiction.*" Contemporary Literature 23* (1982): 323-342.

Denard, Carolyn. "The Convergence of Feminism and Ethnicity in the Fiction of Toni Morrison. McKay, 171-179.

Derrida, Jacques. *Of Grammatology.* Trans. Gayatry Chakravorty Spivak. Baltimore: Johns Hopkins UP, 1976.

Diamond, Irene, and Lee Quinby, eds. *Feminism and Foucault: Reflections on Resistance.* Boston: Northeastern UP, 1988.

Du Bois, W. E. B. *The Souls of Black Folk.* 1903. New York: NAL, 1982.

Ensslen, Klaus. "Fictionalizing History: David Bradley's *The Chaneysville Incident." Callaloo: An African-American and African Journal of Arts and Letters* 11.2 (1988): 280-295.

Escoffier, Jeffrey. "The Political Economy of the Closet: Notes Toward an Economic History of Gay and Lesbian Life Before Stonewall." *Homo Economics: Capitalism, Community, and Lesbian and Gay Life.* Amy Gluckman and Betsy Reed, eds. New York: Routledge, 1997. 123-134.

Ensslen, Klaus. "Fictionalizing History: David Bradley's *The Chaneysville Incident*." *Callaloo: An African-American and African Journal of Arts and Letters* 11.2 (1988): 280-295.

Feinberg, Leslie. Closing speech. Lesbian, Gay, and Bisexual Pride Week. Penn State University. University Park, PA, 11 April, 1994.

———. *Transgender Liberation: A Movement Whose Time Has Come*. New York: Worldview Forum, 1992.

———. *Transgender Warriors: Making History from Joan of Arc to RuPaul*. Boston: Beacon, 1996.

Ferguson, Kathy E. *The Man Question: Visions of Subjectivity in Feminist Theory*. Berkeley: U of California P, 1993.

Foucault, Michel. *Discipline and Punish*. Trans. Alan Sheridan. New York: Vintage, 1979.

———. *Herculine Barbin: Being the Recently Discovered Memoirs of a Nineteenth-Century French Hermaphrodite*. Trans. Richard McDougall. New York: Pantheon, 1980.

———. *The History of Sexuality. Vol. 1: An Introduction*. 1978. Trans. Robert Hurley. New York: Vintage, 1980.

———. "Michel Foucault: Final Interview." *Raritan Review* 5 (1985): 1-13.

———. *Power/Knowledge: Selected Interviews and Other Writings*, 1972-77. Ed. Colin Gordon. New York: Pantheon, 1980.

———. *The Use of Pleasure*. Trans. Robert Hurley. New York: Pantheon, 1985. Vol. 2 of *The History of Sexuality*. 3 vols. 1978-1986.

Franklin, John Hope. *An Illustrated History of Black Americans*. New York: Time-Life Books, 1970.

Friedman, Ellen G. "Where Are the Missing Contents? (Post)Modernism, Gender, and the Canon." *PMLA* 108 (1993): 240-252.

Fussell, Betty. "All that Jazz." *Conversations with Toni Morrison*. Ed. Danille Taylor-Guthrie. Jackson: U P of Mississippi, 1994. 280-287.

Garber, Marjorie. *Vested Interests: Cross-Dressing and Cultural Anxiety*. New York: Routledge, 1991.

Gates, Henry Louis, Jr., and K. A. Appiah eds. *Toni Morrison: Critical Perspectives Past and Present*. New York: Amistad, 1993.

Grosz, Elizabeth. *Volatile Bodies: Toward a Corporeal Feminism*. Bloomington: Indiana UP, 1994.

Heinze, Denise. *The Dilemma of Double Consciousness in Toni Morrison's Novels*. Athens: U of Georgia P, 1993.

Herdt, Gilbert, ed. *Third Sex, Third Gender: Beyond Sexual Dimorphism in Culture and History.* Zone Books: New York, 1994.

Herrnstein, Richard J., and Charles Murray. *The Bell Curve.* New York: Free Press, 1994.

Hite, Molly. "First the Bad News." Rev. of *Lifting a Ton of Feathers: A Woman's Guide to Surviving in the Academic World*, by Paula J. Caplan. *The Women's Review of Books* May 1994: 19.

Hoch, Paul. *White Hero, Black Beast: Racism, Sexism and the Mask of Masculinity.* London: Pluto, 1979.

hooks, bell. *Black Looks.* Boston: South End, 1992.

——. *Sisters of the Yam: Black Women and Self-Recovery.* Boston: South End, 1993.

——. *Yearnings: Race, Gender, and Cultural Politics.* Boston: South End, 1990.

Hoover, Mary Rhodes. "A Vindicationist Perspective on the Role of Ebonics (Black Language) and Other Aspects of Ethnic Studies in the University." *American Behavioral Scientist* 34.2 (1990): 251-262.

Hoy, David Couzens. *Foucault: A Critical Reader.* Oxford: Basil Blackwell, 1986.

Hulbert, Ann. Rev. of *Jazz*, by Toni Morrison. *New Republic* 18 May 1992: 48.

Hume, Kathryn. "Ishmael Reed and the Problematics of Control." *PMLA* 108 (1993): 506-528.

Hutcheon, Linda. *The Politics of Postmodernism.* London: Routledge, 1989.

Hwang, David Henry. "*M. Butterfly*: An Interview with David Henry Hwang." John Louis DiGaetani. *The Drama Review: A Journal of Performance Studies* 33.3 (Fall 1989): 141-153.

Jordan, June. "Seeking an Attitude." *The Women's Review of Books* 10.8 (May 1993): 9-10.

Kauffman, Linda, ed. *Gender and Theory: Dialogues on Feminist Criticism.* Oxford: Basil Blackwell, 1989.

Kristeva, Julia. "Woman Can Never Be Defined." Trans. Marilyn A. August. Marks and de Courtivron, 137-141.

Lamos, Colleen. "Taking on the Phallus." *Lesbian Erotics.* Ed. Karla Jay. New York U P, 1995: 99-119.

Lothstein, Leslie Martin. *Female-to-Male Transsexualism.* Boston: Routledge & Kegan Paul, 1983.

MacKenzie, Gordene Olga. *Transgender Nation*. Bowling Green, OH:
        Bowling Green State University Popular Press, 1994.

Madhubuti, Haki R. *Black Men: Obsolete, Single, Dangerous? Afrikan
        American Families in Transition: Essays in Discovery, Solution and
        Hope*. Chicago: Third World, 1990.

Mann, Patricia S. *Micro-Politics: Agency in a Postfeminist Era*. Minneapolis:
        U of Minnesota P, 1994.

Mariani, Philomena, ed. *Critical Fictions: The Politics of Imaginative
        Writing*. Seattle: Bay Press, 1991.

Marks, Elaine and Isabelle de Courtivron, eds. *New French Feminisms*.
        Amherst: U of Massachusetts P, 1980.

Martin, Wallace. *Recent Theories of Narrative*. Ithaca: Cornell UP, 1986.

McCall, Nathan. *Makes Me Wanna Holler: A Young Black Man in America*.
        New York: Random, 1994.

McDowell, Deborah. "Harlem Nocturne." Rev. of *Jazz*, by Toni Morrison.
        The Women's Review of Books 9.9 (June 1992): 1, 3-5.

McKay, Nellie Y., ed. *Critical Essays on Toni Morrison*. Boston: Hall, 1988.

Means, Russell. "The Same Old Song." Churchill, 19-33.

Minkowitz, Donna. "Love Hurts." *The Village Voice* 19 April 1994: 24-30.

Morgan, Robin. *The Word of a Woman: Feminist Dispatches* 1968-1992.
        New York: Norton, 1992.

Morrison, Toni. *Playing in the Dark: Whiteness and the Literary Imagination*.
        Cambridge: Harvard UP, 1992.

Mullen, Harryette. "Optic White: Blackness and the Production of
        Whiteness." *Diacrites: A Review of Contemporary Criticism* 24.2-3
        (Summer-Fall 1994): 71-89.

Munt, Sally, ed. *New Lesbian Criticism: Literary and Cultural Readings*.
        New York: Columbia UP, 1992.

Nestle, Joan, ed. *The Persistent Desire: A Femme-Butch Reader*. Boston:
        Alyson Publications, 1992.

——. *A Restricted Country*. Ithaca: Firebrand, 1987.

Newton, Esther. *Mother Camp: Female Impersonators in America*. Chicago:
        U of Chicago P, 1972.

Peterson, Nancy J. "History, Postmodernism, and Louise Erdrich's *Tracks*."
        PMLA 109 (Oct. 1994): 982-994.

Jay Prosser. "No Place Like Home: The Transgendered Narrative of Leslie
        Feinberg's *Stone Butch Blues*." *Modern Fiction Studies* 41.3-4
        (1995): 493-512.

Rainwater, Lee, and William W. Yancey. *The Moynihan Report and the Politics of Controversy*. Cambridge, MA: MIT P, 1967.

Ramazanoglu, Caroline, ed. *Up Against Foucault: Explorations of Some Tensions Between Foucault and Feminism*. London: Routledge, 1993.

Ransom, Janet. "Feminism, Difference, and Discourse: The Limits of Discursive Analysis for Feminism." Ramazanoglu, 123-146.

Raymond, Janice G. *The Transsexual Empire*. Boston: Beacon, 1979.

Reed, Harry. "Toni Morrison, Song of Solomon, and Black Cultural Nationalism." *The Centennial Review* 32.1 (1988): 50-64.

Reed, Ishmael. *Airing Dirty Laundry*. Reading, MA: Addison-Wesley, 1993.

Rideau, Wilbert, and Ron Wikberg. *Life Sentences: Rage and Survival Behind Bars*. New York: Times Books/Random, 1992.

Rigney, Barbara Hill. *The Voices of Toni Morrison*. Columbus: Ohio State UP, 1991.

Robinson, Sally. *Engendering the Subject: Gender and Self-Representation in Contemporary Women's Fiction*. Albany: State U of New York P, 1991.

Roscoe, Will. "How to Become a Berdache: Toward a Unified Analysis of Gender Diversity." Herdt, 329-372.

Rothblatt, Martine. *The Apartheid of Sex: A Manifesto on the Freedom of Gender*. New York: Crown, 1995.

Rubenstein, Roberta. "Pariahs and Community." Gates and Appiah, 126-158.

Sando, Joe S. *Pueblo Nations: Eight Centuries of Pueblo Indian History*. Santa Fe: Clear Light, 1990.

Sawicki, Jana. "Feminism and the Power of Foucaldian Discourse." Arac 161-78.

Scarry, Elaine. *The Body in Pain: The Making and Unmaking of the World*. New York: Oxford UP, 1985.

Schwenger, Peter. "The Masculine Mode." *Critical Inquiry* 5 (1979): 621-33. Rpt. in *Speaking of Gender*. Ed. Elaine Showalter. New York: Routledge, 1989. 101-112.

Shakur, Sanyika. *Monster*. New York: Grove: 1993.

Silko, Leslie Marmon. "Language and Literature from a Pueblo Indian Perspective." Mariani 83-93.

——. "A Leslie Marmon Silko Interview." Kim Barnes. *The Journal of Ethnic Studies*. 13.4 (1986): 83-105.

——. "Stories and Their Tellers: A Conversation with Leslie Marmon Silko." Dexter Fisher. *The Third Woman: Minority Women Writers of the*

United States. Ed. Dexter Fisher. Boston: Houghton Mifflin, 1980. 18-23.

Skow, John. "People of the Monkey Wrench." Rev. of *Almanac of the Dead*, by Leslie Marmon Silko. *Time* 9 Dec. 1991, 86.

Smith, Patricia Clark. "Ain't Seen You Since: Dissent Among Female Relatives in American Indian Women's Poetry." *Studies In American Indian Literature: Critical Essays and Course Designs.* Ed. Paula Gunn Allen. New York: MLA, 1983. 108-126.

Snow, Anita. "Mexico, Guerilla Leaders Agree to Hold Formal Talks." *Daily Collegian* 11 April 1995: A3.

Solomon, Alisa. "Identity Crisis: Queer Politics in the Age of Possibilities." *The Village Voice* 30 June 1992: 27-29, 33.

Stone, Sandy. "The Empire Strikes Back: A Posttranssexual Manifesto." *Body Guards: The Cultural Politics of Gender Ambiguity,"* ed. Julia Epstein and Kristina Straub. New York: Routledge, 1991.

Swan, Edith E. "Laguna Symbolic Geography and Silko's *Ceremony.*" *American Indian Quarterly* 12 (Summer 1988): 229-249.

——. "Feminine Perspectives at Laguna Pueblo: Silko's *Ceremony.*" *Tulsa Studies in Women's Literature* 11 (1992): 309-27.

Tallent, Elizabeth. Rev. of *Almanac of the Dead. New York Times Book Review* 22 Dec. 1991, 6.

Trinh, T. Minh-ha. *Woman, Native, Other.* Bloomington: Indiana UP, 1989.

Tyler, Hamilton A. *Pueblo Birds and Myths.* Norman, OK: U of Oklahoma P, 1979.

Van Der Zee, James. *Harlem Book of the Dead.* Dobbs Ferry, New York: Morgan and Morgan, 1978.

Wall, Cheryl A., ed. *Changing Our Own Words: Essays on Criticism, Theory, and Writing by Black Women.* New Brunswick: Rutgers UP, 1989.

Walzer, Michael. "The Politics of Michel Foucault." Hoy 51-68.

Warner, Anne Bradford. "New Myths and Ancient Properties: The Fiction of Toni Morrison." *The Hollins Critic* 25.3 (1988): 1-11.

Washington, Mary Helen. "Black History: His Story or Hers." *Washington Post* 12 April 1981: 3, 13.

Waugh, Patricia. *Feminine Fictions: Revisiting the Postmodern.* London: Routledge, 1989.

White, Hayden. "Getting Out of History." *Diacritics* 12.3 (1982): 2-13.

Williams, Jerome D., et al. " Ebonics and Advertising to the Black Consumer: A Need for Research to Analyze Language and Communication

Styles in Linguistic Framework." *Proceedings of the Thirteenth Annual Conference of the Academy of Marketing Science. Orlando, Florida, May 17-20, 1989.* Vol. 12 of *Developments in Marketing Science.* 16 vols. to date. Marquette, MI: Academy of Marketing Science, 1978-.

Williams, Walter L. *The Spirit and the Flesh: Sexual Diversity in American Indian Culture.* Boston: Beacon, 1988.

Willis, Susan. "Eruptions of Funk: Historicizing Toni Morrison. *Black American Literature Forum* 16.1 (1982): 34-42. (Rpt. in *Toni Morrison: Critical Perspectives Past and Present*, Ed. Henry Louis Gates, Jr. and K. A. Appiah. 308-329.)

——. "I Shop Therefore I Am: Is There A Place For Afro-American Culture in Commodity Culture?" Wall, 173-195.

Wolf, Maxine. "Invisible Women in Invisible Places: The Production of Social Space in Lesbian Bars." *Queers in Space: Communities/Public Places/Sites of Resistance.* Ed. Gordon Brent Ingram, Anne-Marie Bouthillette, and Yolanda Retter. Seattle: Bay Press, 1997. 301-324.

X, Malcolm, and Alex Haley. *The Autobiography of Malcolm X.* New York: Ballantine, 1964, 1965.

Index